# Cursive Stroke Formations

# Penmanship

## for Christian Writing

## Grade 3

### Teacher's Manual

Rod and Staff Publishers, Inc.
P.O. Box 3, Hwy. 172
Crockett, Kentucky 41413
Teleph

*Rod and Staff Books*
(Milestone Ministries)
800-761-0234 or 541-466-3231
**www.RodandStaffBooks.com**

# Acknowledgements

We acknowledge that our omniscient, ever-present Lord has provided us the opportunity and understanding for a venture of this sort. Working closely together, those involved have been enabled by God to establish this new Penmanship series. Our desire has been to please the Lord in providing this course for the Christian school.

We also acknowledge that we have benefited from other handwriting systems in developing the system used in this series. And many teachers were also consulted.

Research and Writing—Daniel Strubhar

Final Editing—Marvin Eicher

## Grade  Three  Curriculum

Pupil's Workbook Units 1, 2
Teacher's Manual

*Copyright, 1982*

Rod and Staff Publishers, Inc.
Crockett, Kentucky 41413

Printed in U.S.A.

ISBN 978-07399-0566-1

Catalog no. 15391

12    13    14    15    16    —    20    19    18    17    16    15    14    13    12    11

# Table of Contents

## Unit 1 Slant Print and Small Cursive Letters

## Unit 2 Cursive Capitals and Writing Quality

# Introduction
# to Penmanship Series

Penmanship is a subject that many teachers have often overlooked. The reasons are many and varied; but no doubt the main reason is simply that other subjects are considered to be more important, and penmanship has been crowded into the background. But we feel that handwriting needs to hold a prominent place in our Christian school curriculums and that it needs to be taught in an orderly, thorough, and efficient manner. This is the basic reason behind the production of this handwriting series.

## The Importance of Teaching Penmanship in Our Schools

1. Good penmanship is a mark of Christina carefulness. God expects His people to be thorough and exact in their activities, not slipshod and careless.

2. Good penmanship is a mark of Christian courtesy. Writing that is difficult to read will not be appreciated by those who must read it.

3. Good penmanship is necessary for good communication. Even though word processors and copiers have taken over in many areas of communication, there are still many purposes for writing that are better accomplished by means of handwriting.

4. Good penmanship is an aid to efficiency. Well-written messages are far less time-consuming to read than those poorly written.

5. Good penmanship will affect students' attitudes. If neat writing is insisted upon, the very act of penning words and sentences in a neat manner will cause students to want to do their best work.

6. Good penmanship on the part of our students will leave a good testimony for our school program. Penmanship is the first thing that impresses the critical eye, before the quality of the work done is apparent.

7. We need to teach good penmanship because it is right. We must do well whatever needs to be done. "Whatsoever thy hand findeth to do, do it with thy might" (Ecclesiastes 9:10).

## Our Approach to Handwriting

### 1. Teaching by Strokes

Teaching handwriting by strokes is the simplest and most efficient way to get the principles of handwriting across. With this approach, the child learns and practices a few basic strokes from which most letters are composed. As he learns these strokes, he has a tool for conquering difficulties in letter formation. In practicing the strokes, he will also become better acquainted with the feel of the basic movements of handwriting, which will help his handwriting to become more efficient and more automatic.

The stroke approach is also beneficial from the teacher's standpoint. It gives him something to teach in handwriting, rather than allowing handwriting instruction to degenerate into nothing more than remedial work. It tends to give a greater enthusiasm for handwriting, because the teacher will know better how to teach it.

Here is how two typical letters are learned by the stroke method:

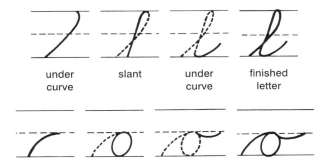

| under curve | slant | under curve | finished letter |

### 2. Teaching Quality

In this course we want to give considerable attention to the teaching of quality. Quality includes slant, alignment, size, proportion, line quality, and spacing, and is a very important part of handwriting (see diagrams and definitions below). The proper teaching of quality may spell the difference between success and failure in teaching handwriting. The teaching of quality should not be too far removed from the teaching of letter form, so that the children do not separate the two in everyday writing.

6

Definitions:

*Slant*—degree to which a letter is slanted

    *consistent slant*—all letters slanted the same

    *correct slant*—straight up and down for first grade manuscript; leaning forward for slant print and cursive

*Alignment*—tops and bottoms of letters in straight lines

*Size*—largeness or smallness of letters in comparison with what they should be (guidelines for size are specific in each grade)

*Proportion*—size of letters or letter parts in relation to other letters or letter parts

*Line quality*—degree of lightness or heaviness of writing, related to pencil pressure

*Spacing*—distance between words, letters, or sentences

Diagrams of the six areas of quality:

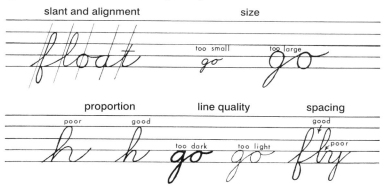

### 3. Difference in Emphasis at Various Grade Levels

In this course, we follow an emphasis at each grade level which builds upon the previous grade, while also reviewing a large part of the previous year's material. The first three grades contain the bulk of new material. For this reason, these grades are the most basic, and the teachers of these grades must be especially careful to give the children a right foundation in handwriting. Grade four contains the least new material. Quality should receive a greater emphasis in grades four to six, and the teachers of these three grades must put forth a continuous effort to keep the students' handwriting up to the standard. In seventh and eighth grades, teachers must emphasize speed, efficiency, and practical handwriting applications in everyday life, while still continuing an emphasis on handwriting quality.

# Posture, Pencil Holding, and Paper Placement

Following are standards for proper posture, pencil holding, and paper placement:

1. Posture at seat
   a. Sit back in the seat.
   b. Sit up straight.
   c. Have feet flat on the floor.
   d. Lean slightly forward from the hips.
   e. Have one arm on desk, holding paper, while the other arm writes.

**POSTURE**

*Sit and stand with your back straight and with both feet flat on the floor. Lean forward only a little when you sit at your desk.*

2. Posture at blackboard
   a. Stand squarely on both feet directly in front of the blackboard.
   b. Stand back six to twelve inches from the blackboard.

3. Pencil holding
   a. Pencil should be held between the thumb and first finger, resting lightly on the second finger.
   b. Pencil should be held no more firmly than necessary for control.
   c. Pencil must not be cramped or pinched.
4. Chalk holding
   a. Chalk should be held pinched-pencil style, firmly between thumb and first two fingers.
   b. Chalk should point toward the palm of the hand.

 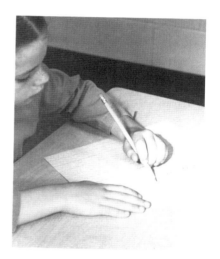

**PENCIL HOLDING**

*Hold the pencil so that its top points back over your shoulder. Hold it tightly enough to control it, but do not pinch it.*

5. Paper placement
   a. For slant print and cursive writing, right-handers should slant the paper about thirty degrees to the left, and left-handers should slant it toward the right as taught in "Special Instructions for Left-handed Pupils."

b. The paper should be on the side of the desk toward the arm that will be used to write.

 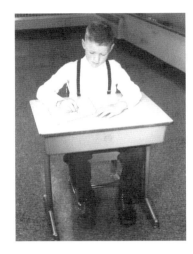

**PAPER PLACEMENT**

*If you write with your right hand, slant the paper to the left. If you write with your left hand, slant the paper to the right far enough so that you can see your writing.*

# Special Instructions
# for Left-handed Pupils

Many teachers seem confused when it comes to teaching left-handed pupils how to write. How should they slant their papers and hold their pencils? How can they write so as to be able to see their writing? How does one prevent them from developing a hooked wrist? This section is intended to answer these questions with sound, positive directions for teachers of left-handers. Although some points may seem strange and even impractical, note carefully that these *principles were developed over several decades* of experimentation with left-handers in many schools. Those left-handers who learned to write by this method developed a neater, more even, and more efficient handwriting style than those taught by other methods. Therefore, unless your left-handed students have already formed poor writing habits, these principles will practically guarantee success if you diligently follow them.

A left-handed pupil must deal with a peculiar handicap when he learns to write. Writing moves from left to right; and for the left-handed person, this means that his writing hand will cover his writing as he moves along. Therefore, many left-handers resort to what seems the simplest solution: a hooked wrist.

However, the hooked wrist is by no means the best solution to this problem. This method makes writing laboriously slow, inefficient, and unpleasant. A far better method is to teach left-handed pupils *from the start* that there are certain things they must do differently from right-handed pupils if they are to write well. These differences are listed here.

1. Instead of placing their papers vertically (or slanted to the left for cursive) on their desks, *left-handers must always slant their papers to the right.* In first grade their arms should meet the lines of their papers at right angles; later, *for cursive writing,* their arms should meet their papers *across the lower right-hand corner.* Although this much slant may seem extreme, experience has shown that this is the best way for left-handers to get the proper slant on their letters without using a hooked wrist.

2. *Left-handers should always write toward, not away from, themselves.* If they slant their papers properly, as outlined in number 1 above, they will naturally do this. But when they write at

the blackboard, you will need to make special provisions so that this is possible. *Therefore, give a left-handed child about twice as much room at the blackboard* as what you give to a right-handed child. Then, instead of writing in the space directly in front of him, he can start in the space to his left and write *toward himself* as a left-handed writer should.

3. *Left-handers should hold their pencils exactly the same way that right-handers do.* If they cannot see their writing, either they are holding the pencil too close to the point or their desks are too high. Left-handers can normally write better at a desk lower than usual, because they can better see over their writing hand that way.

4. *If you have a large number of left-handers, group them together* for penmanship classes if possible. This would be especially good in the lower grades, where handwriting habits are first being established. In this way they will not become confused as easily by the right-handers, and you can more quickly see whether they are developing proper habits. Place this group to the right side of the class (as you face the front) so that they can read, as well as write, *toward themselves.*

5. In slant printing and cursive writing, the left-hander's strokes are opposite of the right-hander's. The right-hander *pulls* downstrokes vertically *toward himself,* whereas the left-hander should *push* downstrokes horizontally *away from himself.* Also, the right-hander *pushes* across strokes horizontally away from himself, but the left-hander should *pull* across strokes vertically *toward himself.* Study this diagram carefully:

| Left-hander | Right-hander |
|:---:|:---:|
| 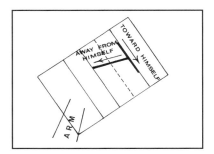 | 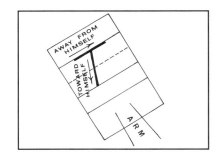 |

12

Again, do not be surprised if you have never heard of some of these points. Perhaps *your* teachers never heard of them either! Begin *now* to put them to use. Then you will have the satisfaction of teaching by a definite method that works, and you will have begun on the road to successful handwriting for your left-handed pupils.

Illustrations for proper pencil holding, paper placement, and writing method for left-handed pupils are included in the section "Posture, Pencil Holding, and Paper Placement."

# How to Treat the Teacher's Manual

In this course there are detailed teacher's instructions for each lesson, gving direction to the teacher about goals to strive for, how to fill out the workbooks, and how to conduct the class so that the children gain the clearest possible understanding of the lesson. Other diagnostic, remedial, and informative suggestions are given, and each lesson has a reduction of the student workbook lesson, for the teacher's handy reference.

We suggest that you as a teacher do not overlook the teacher's daily instructions in your preparation for class, but that you study them carefully sometime previous to the class period. Especially the inexperienced teacher should read them carefully and thoroughly. Do not let your teaching flounder because of a lack of understanding of the subject material and correct class procedure. Even an experienced teacher does well to study the teacher's manual, although he may already be able to teach the writing of the alphabet successfully. It will help him to understand the approach we are taking in the teaching of this course, and the sequence of thought throughout the lessons.

We suggest not only that you read the directions for each lesson a few hours previous to teaching it, but also that you read ahead in the teacher's manual from time to time, to keep abreast of just where you are in accomplishing your goals for the year. You may also find that some of the suggestions given in future lessons may be helpful to you in the lessons you are presently teaching, even though they may not always be directly applicable to the present lesson.

Do not take for granted that just because something is not mentioned in the directions for a particular lesson, it is therefore not to be considered in that lesson. For example, not every lesson mentions that you should be sure your children practice correct posture and pencil-holding habits, but you should watch for this each day. Various items of this nature will be brought to your attention from time to time as reminders to keep watching these areas.

Finally, do not be a slave to your teacher's manual. You do not have to accept every suggestion or follow the exact procedure for every class period that is outlined, right down to saying the exact words that are suggested. The teacher's manual is available to guide the teacher's thinking and is not the final rule of procedure for every situation. However, the basic suggestions were included because they were felt to be important, and the teacher should consider and use them in one form or another as he plans the lesson.

# To the Third Grade Teacher

Because of the cursive foundations laid in third grade, it is certainly of at least equal importance with Grades 1 and 2. Build solidly and well upon the cursive foundation already established in second grade; it would be good for you to study the second grade teacher's manual if you are not familiar with it. Following are some building blocks that you will want to use in accomplishing your task with third grade.

1. *Maintenance of correct habits of posture, pencil holding, and paper placement.* Reestablish these habits promptly at the beginning of the year, and maintain them throughout the year.

2. *A good teacher example.* You should have good handwriting yourself. It will be difficult for you to teach good handwriting with any degree of success unless you are able to apply handwriting principles to your own handwriting. Be willing to teach yourself good handwriting if necessary. You may even find it beneficial to do each lesson in a student's book before you teach it.

3. *A good emphasis on review.* You should be making sure that your children retain what they have been learning by emphasizing continual review. Even when the lesson does not have a line of review as such, it would be well for you to take a few minutes to have them practice a formerly learned letter or stroke.

4. *Teaching each lesson well.* Never be satisfied until you are quite certain that the children are doing the best they can.

5. *Not allowing significantly poorer work in daily assignments in other subjects than in the writing lesson.* The children must understand that what they learn in penmanship class is to be applied in other subjects. You could even take an occasional penmanship grade from another subject, being sure to mark the errors so that the grade is meaningful.

## Textbook Organization and Goals

This textbook has sixty lessons and is organized into two units. Each unit contains thirty lessons. The first unit deals with manuscript writing review and thoroughly reteaches the formation of the small cursive letters. The second unit teaches the cursive capitals and pursues the application of quality in handwriting, which is accomplished in part by combining some strokes together. Combining strokes is also conducive to improvement of overall letter style and increased speed.

You will notice that the manuscript taught in third grade is slanted. Slant print was introduced in second grade as a transition from manuscript to cursive, and it will continue to be the manuscript taught in this course. Slant print permits the exercise of natural hand and arm movements (as cursive writing does), and it is a more relaxed and rapid method of printing than vertical manuscript is.

The main goal of third grade is to give the children a thorough knowledge of cursive writing. A subsidiary goal is to improve the quality of the children's writing.

You will notice that the theme of the book which runs concurrently with the teaching of handwriting is a study of birds. This study is primarily to lend interest to the writing material, and is not intended to be a study in itself. Be sure you do not end up spending more time talking about the birds than you do giving handwriting instruction and training. This could especially be a temptation to one who is nature-minded and not too penmanship-minded. Call brief attention to one interesting facet of the bird that illustrates the day's lesson, and then have the children learn the rest by writing about it. If it is desirable to study birds in the order and manner given in this book, that should not be directly a part of the penmanship class.

**Note:** *The final test is the last lesson in the pupil's book. It should be removed before the books are passed to the students.*

## Time Spent in Writing Class

The textbook is designed for two lessons per week for thirty weeks. This is not a full school year, but it is to aid you in having plenty of time to teach each lesson well and get finished with the book. The lessons should be evenly spaced in the week with approximately the same amount of time between each lesson. The children should be given one of the practice sentences (based on the bird study) to write each morning as a warm-up exercise on the days that you do not have penmanship class. Also, the children can be permitted to finish some lessons outside of class period if necessary.

Allow from 15 to 20 minutes for each class. Yes, it does take time, but third grade is also a basic learning grade. Combining grades at this level yet is discouraged. Take time to be sure the pupils are learning well.

## Conducting the Class

You should follow this basic procedure in teaching the letters of each lesson:

1. *Explain and demonstrate the letter on the blackboard.*
2. *Have the children practice the letter themselves* in the air, on the blackboard, or on other paper as soon as possible after your demonstration.
3. If there is a *"Drill"* section in the lesson, that should come after practice.
4. *The children should work the lesson under your supervision.* Try to correct mistakes when you notice them.
5. *If you are not satisfied with the children's work, keep them practicing* until their work does come up to that which you consider satisfactory.

## What Kind of Work Should You Expect?

The third grader should be expected to do excellent work with slant print if he learned to write with Grades 1 and 2 of this series. Otherwise, he will have to copy the letters as best he can until he learns them well. After a bit of introduction, he should be able to do fair work with cursive small letters, though yet a bit slow. By the end of the year, his ability with cursive capitals ought to be fair. His speed with cursive small letters should have increased, and there should be a definite improvement in quality, such as proper slant, alignment, spacing, and so forth.

At no time should any major deviation from standard form be allowed. Remember, though, that the third grader will not likely have perfectly smooth writing. There will be a few wavers, jiggles, and other irregularities. Try to help the pupils write as smoothly as possible.

## Evaluation and Grading

Evaluation involves looking over your child's paper for errors in form, neatness, and quality. It involves noting the errors you see, so that the child can see what is wrong with his work and how to improve.

You will notice that after Lesson 38 most of the lessons have an evaluation chart. This chart is explained in the teacher's comments of the lesson in which it is introduced. Use it, as it is the most accurate method of grading a lesson, especially for quality. It gives guidelines to help you in giving the child a fair grade for his work.

Prior to the introduction of evaluation charts, follow the same grading procedure as used in second grade, which is: Count neatness as 25 points of the grade, quality as 25 points, and letter formation as 50 points. Subtract points for each area in which there are errors or inaccuracies as you check the pupils' work. Grade the children on how well they are picking up the material and also on their mastery of the three important areas of writing: form, quality, and neatness.

Establish good standards for grading. Do not fall into the habit of giving an *A+* for a excellent paper, an *A* for an average paper, and an *A−* for a poor paper. This is poor grading. Make your grades mean something. If your children's grades are all in the very high bracket, or in the very low bracket, something may be wrong with your grading system.

## Miscellaneous Helps

1. As an aid to your children when they practice on the blackboard, you should draw lines for them to write on. The simplest way is to use a music scorer. For third grade size writing, you do not need to remove any chalk.

Another possibility is to use a felt-tip marker to make the lines. These lines will likely last for a fairly long period of time (a number of months), so you should possibly consult your school board before doing this.

2. Do not forget to use the reverse side of each lesson if you feel that your children need extra practice on paper. If more paper is needed, consider getting paper that has lines which are similar to the lines in this course (available from Rod and Staff).

3. Help the children make the adjustment from paper with guiding lines to paper that has only a bottom line, as in other subjects besides penmanship. Explain to them that they need to estimate the correct height when there are no guide lines. They should try to make the letters proportioned the same as when the guiding lines are there.

# Unit 1

## Slant Print
## and
## Small Cursive Letters

Lessons 1–30

# Lesson 1
# Introduction

**Lesson 1  Introduction**

Reminders:
Are you holding your pencil correctly?
Are you sitting up straight?
Is your paper slanted correctly?

Why did God create birds? The Bible says, "Thou hast created all things, and for thy pleasure they are and were created." God wants us to enjoy birds too.

*Copy each sentence twice.*

We enjoy watching birds fly.

We like to hear their songs.

*Can you answer the question, Why did God create birds? Write a sentence answer below in cursive writing.*

5

## Aim of the Lesson

To introduce the workbook; to reactivate penmanship habits that may have become dormant over the summer.

## Drill

Have the children write the small letters of the alphabet in slant print at the blackboard.

## Conducting the Class

1. If you choose, call attention to the fact that we plan to talk quite a bit about birds this year in penmanship. Read or have a child read the paragraph in the upper right corner.

2. Ask the children to tell you what they can remember about the strokes of cursive writing. Discuss them very briefly.

3. Explain that their cursive writing will be smaller this year than last year. Have them notice the size reduction from last year in line four.

4. Show that cursive writing this year will be three spaces high rather than two spaces as before; however, the spaces are much smaller. The children are not to write their cursive letters up to the top line but only to the third line.

5. Tall letters are three spaces high, short letters are one space high, and the letters *d, p,* and *t* are two spaces high.

## Other Comments

1. Answer to question on last line should be "God created birds for His pleasure," "God created birds for us to enjoy," or some similar statement. These questions are to be answered in complete sentences.

2. You should evaluate this lesson with the aim of seeing where the children are in their penmanship skills. By doing this you will know how rapidly to move ahead.

3. Tell the children to be sure to pay attention to the reminders in the upper left corner of each lesson. Illustrate correct posture, paper placement, and pencil holding (see inside front cover). And they shall *follow directions carefully.*

## Practice Sentences

1. Birds help to make the earth pleasant.
2. Nature is a gift from God.
3. Thank God for our beautiful world.

# Lesson 2
# Multiple Ovals
# and "Ups and Downs"

**Lesson 2    Multiple Ovals
and "Ups and Downs"**

Reminders:
Let your hand move smoothly on the paper
as you form the ovals and "ups and downs."
Do not go above the third line when you
write the sentences.

*Fill these two rows with ovals.*

God has made birds different from other
animals in several ways. One is that most of
them have beaks, which they use to eat food.
Can you think of others?

*Fill these two rows with "ups and downs."*

*Write the first sentence of the paragraph about birds. Then write another way birds are different from other animals.*

7

## Aim of the Lesson

To perfect the children's ability to make multiple ovals and "ups
and downs" neatly and accurately.

## Drill

Have the children practice both multiple ovals and "ups and downs"
at the blackboard and in the air. Be sure they make their movements
large and distinct.

## Conducting the Class

1. Explain to the children that in practicing these drill strokes, they are making all the basic movements that they use in writing cursive letters. Make one copy each of multiple ovals and "ups and downs" on the blackboard to show the children how they are to be done (eight or ten in each set).

2. Conduct drill (see above).

3. Draw a single oval and a single slant. Demonstrate from which parts of each of these that several important strokes of cursive writing are taken (see illustration following "Other Comments"). Explain how all the strokes that comprise the letters of the cursive alphabet are made in some way from these two basic forms.

4. Have the children proceed with the lesson. Go over "Reminders" with them.

## Other Comments

1. The children should read the paragraph in the upper right corner before doing the last part, and think of a correct answer. Their answer will likely be that birds have feathers or wings or that most birds fly. This part should be written in cursive. (If any of them have never learned cursive or have forgotten it, have them print their answer as neatly as possible.)

2. Continue to evaluate the children's writing. Are they gaining back any ground that they may have lost over the summer months?

| slant | retrace | oval | undercurve | overcurve |

# Lesson 3
# Undercurve, Overcurve,
# and Slant Strokes

---

**Lesson 3  Undercurve, Overcurve,
and Slant Strokes**

The robin is well known in North America. It is a medium-sized bird and is very handsome. A young robin has a spotted breast. Look for one next spring!

Reminders:
    Are you sitting up straight?
    Let your whole hand move, not just your fingers, as you write these strokes.
    Do not let your writing go above the third line.

*Fill the row with neat undercurves.*

*Fill this row with overcurves.*

*Fill this row with slants.*

*Copy this sentence twice.*

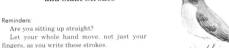

The robin sings a cheerful song.

*Answer below in cursive writing: What is a good way to tell if a bird is a robin?*

9

---

## Aim of the Lesson

To reacquaint the children with the undercurve, overcurve, and slant strokes of cursive writing; and to help them to make them smoothly.

## Drill

Have the children make multiple ovals and "ups and downs" in the air for warm-up. Then they should practice the undercurve, the overcurve, and the slant on the blackboard by retracing back and forth on each stroke as you count to eight.

## Conducting the Class

1. Discuss the three strokes of this lesson by saying that they are the three most frequently used strokes of cursive writing. Therefore, the children should learn to make them well.

2. Demonstrate the three strokes, repeating each stroke several times to show the children how it should be made evenly and smoothly. Again call attention to how the undercurve and overcurve are made from the oval.

3. Conduct drill.

4. Go over the "Reminders" in the upper left corner with the children.

5. Have the children proceed with the lesson, reminding them to follow instructions carefully. They should ask for help if they do not understand any of the instructions.

## Other Comments

1. The answer to the last line will likely be that a robin has a red breast.

2. The value of a line like the last line of this lesson is that it puts the children's writing on a practical level. Most of their writing will be original writing, not simply copied writing. Their original writing should be just as neat as their copied writing.

3. Especially check lines five, six, and seven; and help the children with any special cursive problems you notice in their work.

## Practice Sentences

1. Robins are often found around farms and orchards.
2. The nest of a robin holds four eggs.
3. Robins eat earthworms, bugs, and fruit.

# Lesson 4
# *A, B,* and *C* in Slant Print;
# Numerals *1, 2, 3*

Reminders:
   Is your paper slanted properly?
   Let your hand and arm glide smoothly across
the paper as you write.

Have you ever heard the soft twitter of a
barn swallow on a summer day? God has made
the barn swallow an unusual bird. Below are
two things that make him different.

*Trace each letter, and copy it in the space that follows.*

A                                                    a

B                                                    b

C                                                    c

*Copy the words once on the line below.*

fork  tail        mud  nest

*Copy each numeral in the space following.*

1              2                    3

*Can you guess how the barn swallow got its name? Write your answer below in cursive.*

11

## Aim of the Lesson

To review the formation of the capital and small letters *A*, *B*, and *C* in slant print and also the numerals *1*, *2*, and *3*.

## Drill

Have the children practice the slant print form of the backward-slanting, down, and forward-slanting lines several times at the blackboard.

## Conducting the Class

1. Explain to the children that the kind of printing they will be working with this year is slant print. They should not use the regular vertical manuscript.

2. Review the strokes of slant print: down, up, backward-slanting (b-s), forward-slanting (f-s), across, oval, and curve. See "Other Comments," number 3, for illustration.

3. Conduct drill.

4. The children should practice the capital and small letters *A, B,* and *C* on the blackboard. Help them with correct formation.

5. Go over "Reminders" with the children.

6. Have them proceed with the lesson, following directions carefully.

## Other Comments

1. The barn swallow got its name because it often builds its nests in barns.

2. Especially watch the children's formation of the letters *B* and *C.*

3. Here are the slant print strokes:

down    up    b-s   f-s     across    oval   curve

4. The stroke formations for the above letters are as follows:
   A—f-s line, b-s line, across
   a—oval, up, down
   B—down, across, curve, across; across, curve, across
   b—down, oval
   C—large curve
   c—small curve

5. Emphasize the numerals' formation. The children should make each one neatly with straight lines and smooth-flowing curves.

# Lesson 5
# Round-top and Sharp-top Forms

**Lesson 5    Round-top and Sharp-top Forms**

Reminders:
  Make your round tops round and your sharp tops sharp.
  Are you holding your pencil correctly?

The striking thing about the blue jay is its beautiful coloring of blue, white, and black. It also has a loud call in which it seems to say its name—*jay, jay, jay.*

*Trace the sharp-top and round-top combinations; then copy them in the space that follows each one.*

*Copy this sentence on the line below.*

Blue jays like to pester owls and foxes.

*How is the blue jay like one kind of stroke combination on this page? Answer below in cursive.*

13

## Aim of the Lesson

To teach the children to combine the undercurve and overcurve strokes with the slant stroke to make round-top and sharp-top forms.

## Drill

The children should make round- and sharp-top forms both in the air and on the blackboard over and over until they have acquired a feel for them. Use your own judgment as to when you feel they have sufficient skill in making them.

## Conducting the Class

1. Discuss the round- and sharp-top combinations. Explain that a round top is made with an overcurve and a slant; a sharp top is made with an undercurve and a slant. These combinations are used over and over in writing.

2. Demonstrate these combinations on the blackboard, emphasizing the smoothness of the motions. Carefully explain that these are not primarily finger motions, but rather they are hand and arm motions. Emphasize that the round top should not have a point at the junction of the overcurve and the slant. Neither should its top be so rounded that the slant becomes curved. The children should learn to discern what a desirable joining of these two strokes looks like.

3. Conduct drill, being sure the children make the smooth-flowing movement that is necessary for these forms.

4. Go over "Reminders" with the children.

5. Have them proceed with the lesson according to the directions.

## Other Comments

1. The answer to the question in the last line should be something like: The blue jay's crest is like a sharp top. Tell the children to observe the picture if they do not know the answer right away.

2. What you are really trying to do in this lesson and the following one is to give the child a feel for these stroke combinations that will carry over into his writing of letters and words. One of the keys to good handwriting is getting the overcurve-slant and undercurve-slant combinations to maintain a distinct curve and a distinct slant, so that the curves do not become straight or the slants curved. *This is a very important key to good handwriting.* Failure in getting this principle across in the children's writing is the cause of much poor-quality writing. Do not hesitate to have the children practice and practice and practice some more on these basic stroke combinations.

## Practice Sentences

1. The barn swallow flies very well but almost never walks.
2. The Steller's jay is the blue jay of the West.
3. Blue jays have helped to plant forests by burying nuts.

# Lesson 6
# Round-bottom
# and Sharp-bottom Forms

**Lesson 6  Round-bottom
and Sharp-bottom Forms**

Reminder:
  Be sure your letters and strokes all touch the
bottom line, but do not go below it.

If you hear a sound early some morning like
someone softly sobbing, it may be only a bird—
the mourning dove. It gets its name from its
mournful cooing.

*Trace each stroke combination, and copy it in the space that follows.*
*Round bottoms*

/ U U                                              ℓ ℓ

*Sharp bottoms*

/ ſ ſ                                              ƚ ƚ

*Round tops*                                       *Sharp tops*

∩                    ∩                 ∕              ∕

*Copy the following sentence in cursive.*

*Mourning doves, like all birds in the pigeon*

*family, feed their young by regurgitation.*

15

## Aim of the Lesson

To teach the children to make the round- and sharp-bottom stroke
combinations effortlessly and well.

## Drill

The children should practice the sharp-top and round top stroke
combinations on the blackboard as you count strokes for them (one,
two; one, two; one, two; etc.). Place the accent on the first stroke of

each combination. Have them also practice the round- and sharp-bottom strokes in the air, then on the blackboard or on paper until they have acquired the feel of making them.

## Conducting the Class

1. Explain that a round-bottom combination is made with a slant and an undercurve; a sharp-bottom combination is made with a slant and an overcurve.

2. Demonstrate these combinations on the blackboard, emphasizing again their flowing movement and the importance of using the arm as well as the hand to make them on paper.

3. Be especially diligent in teaching the round-bottom form correctly. The children should leave a point at the bottom of the slant before going on to the undercurve ( $\boldsymbol{\nu}$ , not $\boldsymbol{\omega}$ ). Although it may seem extreme to make this much of a point at the junction of these two strokes, it is good to drill it that way when practicing this combination by itself. Otherwise, it will tend to become overly rounded and formless when the children use it in forming letters.

4. Conduct drill, emphasizing the need for clear, distinct, and smooth movement in making these combinations.

5. Go over the "Reminder" in the upper left corner of the page with the children.

6. Have the children proceed with the lesson according to the directions.

## Other Comments

1. Explain the word *regurgitation* to the children. It means to bring back partly digested food from the stomach to the mouth, from whence, in bird families, the parent birds feed it to the young birds. This long and unfamiliar word will help you to see whether the children can read cursive writing well enough to copy it accurately.

2. If you have time, go through the sentence with the children, having them pick out the sharp-top, round-top, sharp-bottom, and round-bottom combinations. This will help them to see how these forms are used in writing letters and words.

# Lesson 7
# Double Curves, Loops, and Retraces

**Lesson 7 Double Curves, Loops, and Retraces**

Reminders:
Be sure you give both parts of each double curve the same amount of curve.
Are you sitting up straight?

The black-capped chickadee is like the blue jay in one way. It says its name—*chickadee-dee-dee-dee*. It is a very small friendly bird, yet it is the enemy of insect pests, upon which it feeds.

*Trace each combination, and copy it in the space following.*

*Copy this sentence on the line below.*

Chickadees prefer wooded areas.

*What does the first part of this bird's name tell you about it? Write your answer below.*

17

## Aim of the Lesson

To teach the children proper formation of double curves, loops, and retraces.

**Drill** *(to be given before each lesson from here on unless otherwise noted)*

Have the children practice round and sharp tops and bottoms on the blackboard, slowly at first and then more rapidly. Be sure that they maintain neatness.

## Conducting the Class

1. Call attention to each of the three forms to be learned. Give examples of letters that contain each one.

> double curve—*S, T,* and *F*
> large loop—many capitals begin with it—like *H, K, M,* and *N*
> small loop—*E, Z*
> retrace—*b, v,* and *w*

2. Demonstrate these forms, and have the children practice each after you explain it (see "Other Comments," number 3 below, for stroke descriptions). Explain also the backward loop, as in the letter *C,* which is reversed from the regular large loop.

3. Have the children pick out as many of these forms as they can in the sentence on line five.

4. Go over "Reminders" with the children; then have them proceed with the lesson.

## Other Comments

1. The answer for the question above the last line is that the chickadee has a black cap on its head. Answer is to be written in cursive.

2. Take special notice of the fact that the bottom part of the large loop reaches down two-thirds of the way to the bottom line with three-space writing rather than halfway as before.

3. The actual stroke formation of these combinations is as follows:

> double curve—overcurve, undercurve
> loop (variation of oval)—undercurve, overcurve
> small loop—two overcurves or two undercurves ( *ϑ* ) with small loop
> between
> retrace—undercurve, short slant, undercurve

## Practice Sentences

1. The mourning dove flies swiftly and straight.
2. Chickadees are very friendly and cheerful.
3. Chickadees travel in small flocks.

# Lesson 8
# *D*, *E*, and *F* in Slant Print

**Lesson 8** *D, E*, and *F* **in Slant Print**

Reminders:
  Are all of your letters resting firmly on the bottom line?
  Look for round tops, sharp tops, round bottoms, and sharp bottoms, and make them correctly.

A flock of large, white birds among a herd of cows in a pasture—what are they? Most likely they are cattle egrets. Cattle egrets eat insects that bother the cows.

*Copy each letter in the space following.*

D                                          d

E                                          e

F                                          f

*Copy the following sentence in cursive writing.*

Long ago egrets were killed in large

numbers for their beautiful feathers.

19

## Aim of the Lesson

To review the formation of the capital and small letters *D*, *E*, and *F* in slant print.

## Drill

Have the children practice making the across line straight by drawing back and forth on one several times on the blackboard. Also have them practice large top-to-bottom curves and small ovals.

## Conducting the Class

1. Review the stroke formation of each of these six letter forms. Draw the letters on the board stroke by stroke as the children tell you which stroke comes next (refer to the stroke formations in "Other Comments," number 2 below, if necessary).

2. The children should practice these letters on practice paper or in the air, following your discussion of them.

3. On the blackboard the children should write the words *yellow bill* and *short neck* as slant print practice. (These are characteristics of the cattle egret.)

4. Go over "Reminders" and have the children proceed with the lesson.

## Other Comments

1. In talking briefly about the cattle egret, mention the wisdom of God in providing cattle egrets for cows. The South is the home of the cattle egret, and there are also many insect pests in the South.

2. Following are the stroke formations for the letters above:

   *D*—down, across, curve, across

   *d*—oval, up, down

   *E*—down, across, across, across

   *e*—across, curve

   *F*—down, across, across

   *f*—curve, down, across

3. Give the children's cursive sentence in rows five and seven a thorough evaluation. Do you think your students are forming cursive as well as they should be at this point? What areas need improvement? They should be improving to some degree simply through practice of the various strokes and combinations. Soon they will be concentrating more on the formation of individual letters. Then it will be your responsibility to see that they make these stroke combinations practical to their own personal writing.

# Lesson 9
# Small Cursive *i* and *e*

Reminders:
   Remember the dot above every *i*.
   Make a proper-sized loop in *e*.
   Keep the slant of *e* straight.

The northern shrike likes the weather cold. In the North you may never see him except during the winter. His food is mainly small birds, mice, and insects, which he hangs on thorns, bushes, or barbed wire to eat.

*Trace the strokes, and fill rows one and two with i's.*

*ı ⁄ɩ ∖ɩ ı̇*

*Trace the strokes, and fill rows three and four with e's.*

*ı ℓ ℓ*

*Copy this sentence in row six.*

*Shrikes use their hooked beaks often.*

*Answer below: Why do you think it is against the law to kill a shrike?*

21

## Aim of the Lesson

To teach the proper formation of the small cursive letters *i* and *e*.

## Drill

Have the children drill the undercurve and short slant strokes on the blackboard by making rows of these connected together, first an undercurve, then a slant, then an undercurve, and so forth.

## Conducting the Class

1. Explain that *i* and *e* have the same basic stroke combination. (See "Other Comments," number 1, below.) But *e* forms a small loop at the top, and *i* has a dot above it.

2. Look at *i* first. Describe the stroke formation.

3. Demonstrate the letter *i*. (See number 2 below.)

4. Have the children practice the letter *i* in the air.

5. Describe the stroke formation of *e*.

6. Demonstrate the letter *e*, comparing it with *i*. (See numbers 3 and 4 below.)

7. Have the children practice the letter *e* in the air several times.

8. After you have thoroughly explained these two letters, and the children have practiced them, go over "Reminders" and have them proceed with the lesson.

## Other Comments

1. The stroke formations for *i* and *e* are as follows:

   *i* —undercurve, slant, undercurve, dot

   *e* —undercurve, slant, undercurve

2. Take this opportunity to emphasize the importance of always placing the dot directly in line with the slant of the letter *i*.

3. With the letter e, there are several things you should emphasize. One is the proper size for the loop. The children should make sure that the loop is large enough that it can be easily seen. A slight hook at the top of the undercurve is necessary so that the loop can be formed properly.

4. Also, to make a well-formed loop, they must never bend the slant line of the letter. The curve necessary to make the loop must all be in the first undercurve. Insist on this for every one of the children's *e*'s.

5. The answer to the question on the last line is that the shrike kills mice and insects.

6. Evaluate carefully the formation of the letters learned in each lesson. The children's writing should improve as you insist on their making each letter they have learned this year according to proper form.

7. One point of formation that should be mentioned occasionally is the final stroke. It should touch the first line (one-third of the way up). Do not accept "cut off tails" like this: *c* . But notice a slight variation for most lower-loop letters: *y* .

## Practice Sentences

1. Cattle egrets have been in America since about 1938.
2. The northern shrike has a harsh call and a musical song.
3. Shrikes live mostly in open areas.

# Lesson 10
# Small Cursive *u* and *w*

**Lesson 10  Small Cursive *u* and *w***

Reminders:
  Have both feet on the floor as you write.
  Do not let the retrace come down too far on *w*.
  Make all your curves and slants the same.

Most of us are familiar with the unusual habits of woodpeckers. They use their strong, pointed bills to "talk" with other woodpeckers, to make their nests, and to get food for themselves and their families by digging into tree bark for insects.

*Copy the letters u and w in the space that follows them.*

*u  u  u  u  u*

*u  u  u  u  u  u  u*

*Copy these words on the line below.*

*downy     red-headed     hairy     woodpecker*

*Would woodpeckers rather live in forests or in open country? Answer below.*

*Copy each letter below accurately in the space that follows.*

*i*                    *e*

23

## Aim of the Lesson

To teach the children the proper formation of the small cursive letters *u* and *w*.

## Drill

Have the children drill the retrace combination  (undercurve, retrace, undercurve). The retrace combination should be drilled to a count of one, two, three. Then have them practice the undercurve and slant separately.

## Conducting the Class

1. Look first at the letter *u*. Discuss the stroke formation. (See "Other Comments," number 1, below.)

2. Demonstrate the letter on the blackboard. (See numbers 2, 4, and 5 below.)

3. Have the children practice the letter *u* in the air a number of times.

4. Discuss the stroke formation of *w*. (See number 1 below.)

5. Demonstrate the letter *w* on the blackboard. (See numbers 3–5 below.)

6. Have the children practice the letter *w* in the air.

7. Following your thorough explanation of these two letters and the children's practice of them, go over "Reminders," and have them proceed with the lesson.

## Other Comments

1. The stroke formations for *u* and *w* are as follows:

   *u* —undercurve, slant, undercurve, slant, undercurve

   *w* —undercurve, slant, undercurve, slant, undercurve, retrace, undercurve

2. Try to impress on the children the movement of the letter *u*. This is a very rhythmic letter, and you should help them to find that rhythm in their formation of it.

3. The children should carry the rhythm of the letter *u* over to the letter *w*, which is formed with the same basic sharp-top combinations. However, the children must be careful that the third slant line is only a retrace rather than a full slant.

4. With both of these letters, the children should be sure to make their slant lines come to a point ( *ᐯ* ) every time they join the undercurves.

5. Watch that the children's alignment is accurate, both top and bottom, for each letter.

6. The answer to the question above the sixth line is that woodpeckers would rather live in forests. Discuss briefly how God uses woodpeckers to protect forests from destruction by harmful insects.

# Lesson 11
# G, H, I, and J in Slant Print;
# Numeral 4

**Lesson 11**  *G, H, I,* and *J*
      **in Slant Print; Numeral** *4*

Reminders:
    Are all your manuscript letters slanted the
same?
    Does your paper have the correct slant?

The grouse is a bird that is not often seen,
yet it is quite plentiful if you look at the right
places. In summer you can most likely see one
by walking through a cleared spot in a wooded
area.

*Trace these letters, and copy them in the space following.*

G            g            H

h            I            i

J            j

*Copy this sentence and the numeral 4 on the line below.*

Grouse seldom fly far or fast. 4 4

*Copy this sentence below in cursive.*

All grouse are good runners.

## Aim of the Lesson

To review formation of the capital and small letters *G, H, I,* and *J* in slant print and also the numeral *4*.

## Drill

Have the children drill on large ovals ( *O* ) and small bottom curves ( **U** ) particularly. They should make about ten of each, all properly formed.

44

## Conducting the Class

1. Review the stroke formations of these four letters on the blackboard (eight in all). Have the children tell you the strokes that make up these letters in their proper order. (See stroke formations under "Other Comments" if necessary.)

2. Have the children practice these letters on practice paper or on the blackboard following your discussion of them.

3. Go over "Reminders" with the children and have them proceed with the lesson.

## Other Comments

1. The stroke combinations for the above letters are as follows:
   *G*—large curve, across
   *g*—oval, up, down, curve
   *H*—down, down, across
   *h*—down, up, curve, down
   *I*—down, across, across
   *i*—down, dot
   *J*—down, curve, across
   *j*—down, curve, dot
2. Some things to watch with these letters:
   a. Be sure the oval of *G* is correctly formed.
   b. Be sure the down lines of *g* and *j* are straight, not blended with the curve.
   c. Be sure the children do not forget the dots above *i* and *j*.
   d. The numeral *4* is made with slant and across lines only. Be sure the lines stop and start at the right places.
3. Try not to de-emphasize slant print to the extent that the children feel it does not matter how careful they are with it. Although they are spending more time on cursive writing than on slant print, slant print will not fail to be important as well.

## Practice Sentences

1. Woodpeckers have stiff tails to prop themselves.
2. There are many different kinds of woodpeckers in this country.
3. The grouse often spends winter nights in soft snowbanks.

# Lesson 12
# Small Cursive *l* and *b*

**Lesson 12  Small Cursive *l* and *b***

Reminders:
  Make the slant line come down to a clear
and distinct point.
  Are the loops of *l* and *b* big enough to be easily seen?

Years ago, the bobolink was known as the
ricebird because of its habit of stopping in the
rice fields on its way south in the fall. There it
would feed on the ripening crop, much to the
displeasure of the farmers.

*Trace l and b, and copy them in the space following.*

*ℓ ℓ ℓ*

*ℓ ℓ ℓ ℓ ℓ*

*Copy the following sentence in row five.*

*The bobolink is a beautiful singer.*

*Why did the rice farmers not like the bobolink? Answer below in cursive.*

*Copy the letters below in the space following.*

*w*          *w*

27

## Aim of the Lesson

To teach the children the proper formation of the small cursive letters *l* and *b*.

## Drill

The children should practice tall undercurves and tall slants (as
in *l* and *b*) separately eight times each. Then they should put them
together so that they make a loop, and practice them several times.

## Conducting the Class

1. Explain how the kind of loop found in tall loop letters is formed. Show that the three strokes of *l* are the same you use for *t*, except that with *l* you put a hook ( *)* ) at the end of the undercurve before making the slant. This is what creates the loop of *l*, *b*, and other letters.

2. Discuss and demonstrate the stroke formation of the letter *l* (see numbers 1 and 2 below).

3. Have the children practice the letter *l* in the air several times.

4. Discuss and demonstrate the letter *b*, emphasizing its similarity with *l* and also its retrace combination. (See number 3 below.)

5. The children should practice the letter *b* several times in the air.

6. Go over "Reminders" and have the children proceed with the lesson.

## Other Comments

1. The stroke formations for *l* and *b* are as follows:

   *l*—undercurve, slant, undercurve

   *b*—undercurve, slant, undercurve, retrace, undercurve

2. With *l*, emphasize the importance of making the loop the right size and of crossing the undercurve exactly at the first dotted line. It will take practice for your children to accomplish this without bending the slant.

3. Along with emphasizing the proper formation of the retrace combination in *b*, be sure they form the loop part exactly the same as in the letter *l*. Also be sure that they make the slant-undercurve (round bottom) combination correctly, including a point at the bottom of the slant line before the undercurve is begun.

4. The answer to the question of the sixth line is: the bobolinks destroyed the farmers' crops.

# Lesson 13
# Small Cursive *h* and *k*

**Lesson 13  Small Cursive *h* and *k***

Reminders:
  Be sure to put enough hook on the end of the first undercurve to make the loop the right size.
  Is your paper slanted correctly?

The kingfisher really lives up to its name. It has a king-sized head, and it lives on fish, which it catches from streams, rivers, and lakes with its long, sharp bill.

*Trace h and k, and copy them in the space following.*

*Copy the following sentence on the line below.*

The kingfisher swallows its food headfirst.

*Would you likely find a kingfisher in the middle of a field? Answer with a sentence.*

*Copy these letters in the space following each.*

29

## Aim of the Lesson

To teach the children the formation of the small cursive letters *h* and *k*.

## Drill

The children should practice short overcurves (as in the overcurve of the letter *h*) and short slants a number of times. The two should also be practiced together as a round-top form.

## Conducting the Class

1. Explain to the children that the first parts of $h$ and $k$ are the same as the first parts of $l$ and $b$: all four are tall loop letters. But the last parts of these letters are different.

2. Explain and demonstrate the stroke formation of the letter $h$. (See numbers 1, 3, and 7 below.) Have the children explain the strokes if you wish.

3. The children should practice the letter $h$ in the air several times.

4. Explain and demonstrate the strokes formation of the letter $k$ on the blackboard. (See numbers 1, 4, 5, and 7 below.)

5. Have the children practice the letter $k$ in the air.

6. Go over "Reminders" and have the children proceed with the lesson.

## Other Comments

1. The stroke combinations for the letters $h$ and $k$ are as follows:

*h*—undercurve, slant, overcurve, slant, undercurve

*k*—undercurve, slant, overcurve, undercurve, slant, undercurve

2. Be sure that the first slant and undercurve on both letters cross exactly one-third of the way up.

3. With the letter $h$, the overcurve should separate quickly from the first slant. The tendency is for the letter to look like this ( *h* ), when it should look like this ( *h* ). Be sure to emphasize this point.

4. The letter $k$ is simply a variation of the letter $h$. Instead of proceeding directly with the short slant following the overcurve, a short backward undercurve is made first. Then a very short slant is made to the bottom line with a final undercurve ending the letter.

5. With $k$, be sure the children leave a space between the end of the short undercurve and the overcurve ( *k* not *k* ).

6. The answer to the question above line six is: No, you would find it near the water instead; or, No, you would not likely find it in a field.

7. Be sure the children are making the tall loops of these letters with accuracy and proper movement.

## Practice Sentences

1. Bobolinks may look like large sparrows.
2. Kingfisher nests are often in tunnels in stream banks.
3. Kingfishers have families of six to eight babies.

# Lesson 14
# *K, L, M,* and *N* in Slant Print;
# Numeral 5

**Lesson 14** *K, L, M,* and *N*
in Slant Print; Numeral 5

Reminder:
Do all short letters touch the middle line, and all tall letters touch the top line?

The sandpiper enjoys wading, as many children do. However, the sandpiper does not wade just for fun. He spends his time on the shore, looking for things to eat—insects and small water animals.

*Copy each letter in rows one to four in the space that follows it.*

K                                    k

L                                    l

M                                    m

N                                    n

*On the line below, copy each word once, and the numeral 5 three times.*

purple     rock     sandpiper     5

*What does the sandpiper eat? Answer below in cursive writing.*

31

## Aim of the Lesson

To review the formation of the capital and small letters *K, L, M,* and *N* in slant print and also the numeral 5.

## Drill

Have the children warm up by practicing backward-slanting and forward-slanting lines ( \ / ) as well as small top curves ( ∩ ) as in *m* and *n* in slant print.

## Conducting the Class

1. Review with the children the stroke formations of the small and capital letters *K, L, M, and N.* (See number 1 below.) Use your ingenuity to provide variety in this.

2. The children should practice at least some of these letters on the blackboard before moving into the lesson.

3. Go over the "Reminder" with the children and have them proceed with the lesson.

## Other Comments

1. The stroke formations for these four slant-print letters are as follows:

   *K*—down, forward-slanting (f-s) line, backward-slanting b-s) line

   *k*—down, f-s line, b-s line

   *L*—down, across

   *l*—down

   *M*—down, b-s line, f-s line, down

   *m*—down, up, curve, down, up, curve down

   *N*—down, b-s line, up

   *n*—down, up, curve, down

2. Explain that the words *purple* and *rock* in row five are names of different kinds of sandpipers.

3. The answer to the question in line seven is clearly stated in the paragraph—insects and small water animals.

4. With the two forms of *K,* be sure that the children make the forward-slanting line from the top down, not from the bottom up. The last three strokes of *M* can be made without lifting the pencil.

5. Again be sure the children are not becoming sloppy with slant print writing. Be sure that all joinings and alignment are accurate and that all strokes are formed carefully.

6. Notice that the curve of the numeral *5* rises slightly higher than one-half height. Also be sure that the across line at the top is made *last* and connects well to the rest of the numeral.

# Lesson 15
# Small Cursive *f*

**Lesson 15  Small Cursive** *f*

Reminders:
  Space the words in the sentence the same distance apart.
  Make the bottom loop of *f* slightly shorter and narrower than the top loop.

One thing that makes a finch different from many other birds is its short and thick bill, which it uses to crack hard seeds. Usually the males are brightly colored, but the females are mainly brown and white like sparrows.

*Copy the letter f in rows one and two.*

$\int$ $\int$ $\int$ $\int$

*Copy the following sentence.*

The song of the purple finch is a deep and

beautiful warble.

*Copy these letters in the space following.*

h                      k

*What do finches do with their unusual bills? Answer below.*

33

## Aim of the Lesson

To teach the proper formation of the cursive letter *f*.

## Drill

Have the children practice the long slant and undercurve separately, and then the two in combination as in the middle two strokes of the cursive letter *f*.

## Conducting the Class

1. Discuss the fact that the letter *f* is a tall loop letter like *l* and *k* but that it is the only tall loop letter that also has a bottom loop. This makes it one of the longest letters of the cursive alphabet.

2. Explain and demonstrate the stroke formation of the letter *f*. (See numbers 1–4 below.)

3. Have the children practice the letter *f* in the air and/or on the blackboard.

4. Go over "Reminders" and have the children proceed with the lesson.

## Other Comments

1. The stroke formation of the cursive letter *f* is as follows:

*f* —undercurve, slant, undercurve, undercurve

2. Help the children to get the back of this letter straight. It is a long slant line, and they may easily get it curved.

3. The second point under "Reminders" deserves special attention. Be sure the children make the lower loop slightly smaller than the upper loop of the letter. Also, the length-to-width relationship of each loop should be approximately the same (incorrect: *ƒƒ*; correct: *ƒ* ).

4. The children should be careful that the slant crosses the first undercurve exactly one-third of the way up. The second undercurve (which finishes the bottom loop) should touch the slant directly at the bottom line.

5. Pay special attention in this lesson to the paper placement and hand positioning of your left-handed students. Are they doing their work correctly (as described in the introduction of this book), or have they reverted to awkward methods of writing, such as the hooked-wrist method? You could also use this opportunity to concentrate attention on the posture, pencil-holding, and paper-placement habits of your right-handed students.

6. The answer to the question in row seven is: They crack hard seeds with their bills.

7. Call the children's attention to the fact that the bird in the picture is a purple finch.

## Practice Sentences

1. Sandpipers have short necks, long legs, and long bills.
2. Caged canaries are in the finch family.
3. The purple finch is commonly seen at bird feeders.

# Lesson 16
# Small Cursive *g* and *q*

### Lesson 16  Small Cursive *g* and *q*

Reminders:
  Be sure you do not get g and q mixed up.
  Be sure the bottom parts of all your letters go the same distance below the bottom line.

If you happen to be along a lake shore or coastal marsh in late spring, you may have a chance to see a new family of geese. The father and the mother goose lead the way. From five to nine baby geese may be coming along behind.

*Trace the letters g and q, and copy them in the space following.*

*r  s  q  g*

*r  s  q  q  q*

*Copy the following words.*

*Canada  goose — black  head,  white  cheek*

*Copy these letters in the space following.*

*f*                    *k*

*Where might you see a family of Canada geese? Finish this sentence in cursive: You might see a family of Canada geese . . .*

35

## Aim of the Lesson

To teach the children the small form of the cursive letters *g* and *q*.

## Drill

Have the children drill on the overcurve and oval (as in the letters *g* and *q*) a number of times separately, and then practice them together several times.

## Conducting the Class

1. Explain the nature of the letters *g* and *q* by showing that they are similar. The first three strokes of both letters are identical.

2. Explain and demonstrate the stroke formations of these two letters on the blackboard. (See numbers 1, 4–6 below.)

3. Go over "Reminders" and have the children proceed with the lesson.

## Other Comments

1. The stroke formation of cursive *g* and *q* are as follows:

   *g* —overcurve, oval, slant, overcurve

   *q* —overcurve, oval, slant, undercurve, undercurve

2. The answer to the question of line seven is: along a lake shore or coastal marsh.

3. Pay special attention to letter spacing in line four. Letters should be spaced the same distance from each other; in other words, spacing must be consistent. Watch also for extra-wide or jammed spacing.

4. Be sure the children keep the slant line straight from top to bottom in both of these letters—do not let them curve it to blend with the stroke that follows.

5. Be sure the children are leaving a proper-sized loop at the bottom of each letter—not too wide or too narrow. The loop should extend 1½ spaces below the base line.

6. Be sure they are not getting these two letters mixed up because of their similarity.

# Lesson 17
# O, P, and Q in Slant Print; Numerals 6, 7, 8

**Lesson 17** *O, P,* **and** *Q* **in Slant Print;**
**Numerals** *6, 7, 8*

Reminders:
There are ovals in all of these letters. Do not make them like circles.
Sit up straight.

Another fish-hunting bird besides the kingfisher is the osprey. The osprey is very large, with a wingspread of about 4½ feet. He flies slowly from 50 to 200 feet above a body of water until he sees a fish. Then he dives quickly after it, making a huge splash when he catches it.

*Copy each letter in the space following.*

O        o

P        p

Q        q

*Copy these words once on row five.*

osprey call – loud, clear whistles.

*Copy each numeral in the space following.*

6        7        8

*Which is larger—the osprey or the kingfisher? Answer with a sentence in cursive writing.*

37

## Aim of the Lesson

To review the formation of the capital and small letters *O, P,* and *Q* in slant print and also the numerals *6, 7,* and *8.*

## Drill

Have the children drill primarily on the large and small ovals on the blackboard.

## Conducting the Class

1. Ask the children to name the stroke that five of these six letters have. The answer is the oval. All these letter forms but capital *P* contain a complete oval.

2. Explain briefly and demonstrate (or have different children come to the board and demonstrate) each of these six letter forms. (See numbers 1–4 below.)

3. Have the children practice these letters in the air or on the blackboard several times.

4. Go over "Reminders" and have the e children go ahead with the lesson.

## Other Comments

1. The stroke formations for these six slant-print letter forms are as follows:

   *O*—large oval
   *o*—small oval
   *P*—down, across, curve, across
   *p*—down, up, oval
   *Q*—large oval, b-s line
   *q*—oval, up, down, curve

2. With all the letter forms that contain ovals, be sure the ovals close without gaps between the beginning and ending of each one.

3. Be sure the curve of the letter *P* is drawn as a proper oval curve. In other words, the curve should look like this ( $\mathcal{D}$ ), not like this ( $\mathsf{D}$ ).

4. The three strokes that make the last part of capital P should be blended together, not formed as individual strokes, or the letter will not have the right appearance. These three strokes must be blended together in such a way that there are no "junction points" between the strokes.

5. Be sure spacing is correct between letters in line five.

6. Be sure the curves of numerals *6, 7,* and *8* are smooth and evenly rounded.

7. The answer to the question in line seven is: The osprey is larger.

## Practice Sentences

1. Flocks of geese are often signs of spring and fall.
2. Geese fly in **V**-shaped flocks while traveling.
3. The osprey will not eat a rotten fish.

# Lesson 18
## Small Cursive *j*

**Lesson 18  Small Cursive** *j*

Reminders:
   Do not forget the dot above the *j*.
   Are you making the slant line straight from
top to bottom?

One of the best times to look for juncos is when
there is snow on the ground. Try throwing bread
crumbs or seeds out on the snow some day this
winter. You may be able to draw a number of
these pleasant little birds.

*Trace the letter j, and copy it in rows one and two.*

*j  j  j  j*

*Copy the following sentence.*

*All juncos have pink bills and white outer*

*tail feathers.*

*Copy these letters in the space following.*

*j*           *j*

*What do juncos like to eat? Answer below.*

39

## Aim of the Lesson

To teach the children the formation of the cursive small letter *j*.

## Drill

Have the children practice long slants and overcurves several times
individually, and then practice them together several times as in the
letter *j* ( **/ ⌐ ɟ** ).

## Conducting the Class

1. Begin by comparing the letters j an g. Show how *j* is, in a way, taken from the letter *g* (⁀*g*).

2. On the blackboard, explain and demonstrate the stroke formation of the letter *j*. (See numbers 1–3 below.)

3. Have the children practice this letter in the air as you count out the strokes (one, two, three, four; one two, three, four; etc.).

4. Go over "Reminders" and have the children proceed with the lesson under your careful supervision.

## Other Comments

1. The stroke formation for this cursive letter is as follows:

   *j*—undercurve, slant, overcurve, dot

2. Since this is a lower-loop letter, strongly emphasize keeping the back of the letter straight from top to bottom. The loop should be 1½ spaces long.

3. Another item to mention with the letter *j* is the importance of making the slant and overcurve cross exactly at the bottom line.

4. With the sentence in this lesson, emphasize keeping the slant of the letters as consistent as possible. Each letter should have exactly the same slant as each other letter.

5. The answer to the question in line seven is: Juncos eat seeds and bread crumbs.

# Lesson 19

# Small Cursive z

**Lesson 19  Small Cursive** *z*

Reminders:
   Let your hand and arm move smoothly across the page.
   Space the letters in each word of the sentence the same distance apart.

Cowbirds are good examples of laziness in the bird world. Instead of taking care of their own babies, they lay their eggs in the nests of other birds for them to hatch and raise. The baby cowbirds are greedy and take much of the food that should go to the other birds.

*Trace the letter ℨ, and copy it in rows one and two.*

*ɾ ɹ ℨ ℨ*

*Copy the following sentence.*

*God does not want us to be lazy like the*

*cowbird.*

*Copy these two letters in the space following.*

*b                                                  z*

*What besides laziness is bad about being like a cowbird? Answer below.*

41

## Aim of the Lesson

To teach the children how to form the cursive small letter *z*.

## Drill

Drill on the undercurve and overcurve separately several times each; then have the children practice them together as in the last part of the letter *z*. You should demonstrate exactly how you want the strokes made.

## Conducting the Class

1. As the children drill, explain that the letter *z* is a lower-loop letter but that the loop is made differently from other lower-loop letters. Instead of having a slant line on one side, it has a curved line on both sides, like the combination they are making at the blackboard.

2. Explain and demonstrate the formation of the letter *z*. (See numbers 1–4 below.)

3. Have the children practice the letter *z* in the air several times.

4. Go over "Reminders" and have the children proceed with the lesson.

## Other Comments

1. The stroke formation of the cursive letter *z* is as follows:
*z*—overcurve, slant, hook, undercurve, overcurve

2. The children should not make the hook in this letter too large. Sometimes children's hooks with this letter end up looking something like this: *y*. However, be sure they do put a small hook between the slant and the undercurve.

3. Be sure the children make the round-top part of the letter correctly. Explain  that the first two strokes in this letter are made just like the hump of the letter *h*. Getting the first part correct will help with the formation of the rest of the letter.

4. Be sure that the bottom part of the letter *z* is properly aligned with the top part. Your children's letters should not look like these: *z z z* .

5. The answer to the question in line seven is that the cowbird is also greedy. However, be careful not to make the cowbird "evil," because the Lord gave this bird its instincts.

## Practice Sentences

1. Juncos are birds of the sparrow family.
2. The cowbird walks with an up-tilted tail.
3. The brown-headed cowbird is the most common in North America.

# Lesson 20
# *R, S,* and *T* in Slant Print; Numerals *9, 0*

**Lesson 20**  *R, S,* **and** *T* **in Slant Print;**
**Numerals** *9, 0*

The starling is one of the most common yet most disliked birds in the world. It is bold and noisy and likes to gather in large flocks, especially in cities. The starling changes color from season to season. It is speckled in the winter and shiny black in the summer.

Reminders:
Remember to make the curves of *S* the same size and shape.
Remember to space the letters and words correctly in the sentence below.

*Trace the letters in rows one to three, and copy them in the space following.*

R                                    r

S                                    s

T                                    t

*Copy the following sentence.*

Starlings have strong legs and feet.

*Copy each numeral in the space following.*

9                                    0

*Would you be more likely to see a starling by itself or in a flock? Finish this sentence in cursive: You would be more likely to see a starling . . .*

43

## Aim of the Lesson

To review with the children the formation of the capital and small letters *R, S,* and *T* in slant print and also the numerals *9* and *0.*

## Drill

Have the children practice making double curves on the blackboard both in a slanted direction, as in the letter *S* ( $\mathcal{S}$ ), and in an across direction ( $\sim$ ).

## Conducting the Class

1. Review with the children the stroke formation of these six letter forms on the blackboard.

2. Have the children practice these letters on the blackboard, in the air, or briefly on practice paper before beginning the lesson.

3. Go over "Reminders" and have the children proceed with the lesson.

## Other Comments

1. The stroke formations for these six slant-print letter forms are as follows:

   *R*—down, across, curve, across, b-s line

   *r*—down, up, curve

   *S*—curve, curve

   *s*—curve, curve

   *T*—down, across

   *t*—down, across

2. The answer to the question in line seven is: in a flock.

3. Emphasize the spacing of the words and letters of the sentence in this lesson. Cursive writing is easier to space properly than manuscript writing. Improper spacing in manuscript writing can make the writing really difficult to read.

4. Be sure the numeral *9* is closed. Numeral *0* should simply be a large oval.

# Lesson 21
# Small Cursive *v* and *y*

**Lesson 21  Small Cursive** *v* **and** *y*

Reminders:
  Be sure all your letters have the same slant.
  Be sure the retrace is the same length in each letter *v*.
  Be sure the second slant line in *y* is straight from top to bottom.

What bird do you know that is both very large and very ugly? That bird would likely be the turkey vulture. Yet he can glide so beautifully that it is fun to watch him. But you certainly would not like to eat what he eats, which is dead and rotting animals.

*Trace the letters v and y, and copy them in the space following.*

*v  v  v  v  v*

*v  v  v  y  y*

*Copy the following sentence.*

*Vultures have very good eyesight.*

*Copy the letter y in this line.*

*y*

*What do vultures eat? Answer below.*

45

## Aim of the Lesson

To teach the children the proper formation of the cursive small letters *v* and *y*.

## Drill

Have the children practice the round-top combination ( ∩ ) and the round-bottom combination ( ∪ ) separately, and then put the two together as in the first part of both of the letters *v* and *y*. Be sure the children make the slant lines straight from top to bottom, and be sure there is a junction point between each stroke.

## Conducting the Class

1. Explain that *v* and *y* both begin with the round-top–round-bottom combination of overcurve, slant, and undercurve.

2. Discuss and demonstrate the stroke formation of each of these letters individually on the blackboard, bringing out the critical areas of proper formation. (See numbers 1–3 below.)

3. Have the children practice these letters stroke by stroke in the air.

4. Go over "Reminders" and have the children proceed with the lesson.

## Other Comments

1. The stroke formations for the cursive letters *v* and *y* are as follows:

    *v*—overcurve, slant, undercurve, retrace, undercurve

    *y*—overcurve, slant, undercurve, slant, overcurve

2. With both of these letters, be sure the children are sharply distinguishing between the first slant and the first undercurve, not rounding them together ( $\cup$ ), but making a clear junction point between the two.

3. Be sure the final overcurve of y crosses the slant line exactly at the bottom line on your children's papers.

4. Check your children's line quality. Are they writing too heavily or too lightly? Encourage them to relax pressure if they are writing heavy lines and to increase pressure if they are writing too lightly. Gripping the pencil closer to the point (to make heavier lines) or farther back (to make lighter lines) should also be helpful.

5. The answer to the question in line seven is: Vultures eat dead and rotting animals.

## Practice Sentences

1. The starling can make the calls of other birds.
2. Vultures are sometimes called buzzards.
3. Several vultures together may mean a dead animal is nearby.

# Lesson 22
# Small Cursive *x*

**Lesson 22  Small Cursive** *x*

Reminders:
  Are you holding your pencil too tightly?
  Watch the spacing of letters in each word of
the sentence.

Do you wonder how the waxwing got such a
strange name? It comes from the small pellets
of red wax that form on the tips of the shorter
wing feathers of this bird. No one seems to
know just why they are there, but God knows
why. Cedar waxwings have a crest and are
mostly yellow and brown.

*Trace and copy the letter* $x$ *in the first two rows.*

*Copy the following sentence.*

Waxwings love to eat ripe berries

and cherries.

*Copy the letters below in the space following.*

*What color are waxwings? Answer below.*

47

## Aim of the Lesson

To teach the children how to form the cursive small letter *x*.

## Drill

The children should again practice the round-top—round-bottom
combination of overcurve, slant, and undercurve several times while
you count strokes. They should also practice the forward-slanting line
from slant manuscript writing.

## Conducting the Class

1. Explain and demonstrate how the letter *x* is formed from the strokes practiced in the drill. (See numbers 1–3 below.)

2. Have the children practice making this letter in the air or on the blackboard several times while you supervise them carefully to ensure correctness.

3. Go over "Reminders" and have the children proceed with the lesson according to the directions.

## Other Comments

1. The stroke formation for the cursive small letter *x* is as follows:
   *x* —overcurve, slant, undercurve, f-s line

2. Many problems with the small cursive *x* center around the crossing of the letter. The forward-slanting line should come from the top down and should cross exactly in the middle of the slant line.

3. Be sure the slant line stays properly slanted like this ( *x* ), not like this ( *x* ).

4. Are your students being just as careful with letter formation and the spacing of words and letters in line seven as they are in lines four and five? Line seven is really a better key to their general writing ability than lines four and five, since it cannot be directly copied. Be sure to consider this line an important part of your evaluation.

5. The answer to the question line seven is: They are mostly yellow and brown.

# Lesson 23
# Small Cursive *a* and *d*

**Lesson 23  Small Cursive** *a* **and** *d*

Reminders:
   Be sure all your letters are slanted the same.
   Be sure the top and bottom of each letter touch the right lines.

Which bird has the longest wings of any in the world? That bird is the wandering albatross, with a wingspread of over eleven feet! But you will never see one flying over your house some morning unless you live on a ship or on an island. Albatrosses spend most of their time softly gliding over oceans.

*Trace these letters, and copy them in the space that follows them.*

*r  a  a  a*

*a  a  d  d  d*

*Copy the following sentence.*

*Albatrosses  need  wind  to  fly  well.*

*Copy these letters in the space following.*

*a*                                              *g*

*Why will you not see an albatross flying over your house? Answer below.*

49

## Aim of the Lesson

To teach the children how to form the cursive small letters *a* and *d*.

## Drill

The children should drill on the oval separately several times; also on the oval with a "tail" (upward slant stroke) as found in the letter *d* ( *d* ). The oval with a tail should close properly; this is a principle of accuracy that should be instilled right from the beginning.

68

## Conducting the Class

1. Explain the similarity of formation between the letters *a* and *d*. The only difference between the two is the tail on the oval of the letter *d*, which is an additional slant stroke that goes up to the second line. This also makes the downward slant line (called a "retrace") longer for this letter than for the letter *a*. Demonstrate the stroke formations of the letters *a* and *d* on the blackboard. (See numbers 1–5 below.)

2. Have the children practice these letters in the air or on the blackboard under your supervision.

3. Go over "Reminders" and have the children proceed with the lesson.

## Other Comments

1. The stroke formations for the cursive letters *a* and *d* are as follows:

   *a* —overcurve, oval, slant, undercurve
   *d* —overcurve, oval, slant, retrace, undercurve

2. Watch that the oval is formed properly—neither too round ( *d* ) nor too flat ( *d* ), but properly slanted and shaped.

3. *Insist* right from the start that *a* and *d* be closed at the top. Do not let even one unclosed letter get by.

4. Be sure the downward slant line on the children's *a* and *d* does not follow the oval all the way to the bottom. It should not look like this ( *d* ), but like this ( *d* ).

5. Be sure a loop does not form at the top of the letter *d* between the slant and the retrace line ( *d* ).

6. The answer to the question of line seven is: They live out on the ocean.

## Practice Sentences

1. Waxwings do not fly by themselves, but in large flocks.
2. Some albatrosses have flown around the world.
3. Some albatrosses live to be 36 years old.

# Lesson 24

# *U, V,* and *W* in Slant Print

**Lesson 24** *U, V,* **and** *W* **in Slant Print**

Reminders:
Be sure you are making each letter the same as other letters like it.
Hold your pencil firmly, and let your hand move smoothly across the page.

The swan is one of the most beautiful and graceful birds in God's creation. One unusual thing about the swan is its long neck. It is like a giraffe in the bird world! That long and beautiful neck is very useful to the swan. It helps him to reach food on the bottom of lakes and ponds.

*Copy the letters in rows one to three in the space following.*

U                                    U

V                                    V

W                                    W

*Copy the words in rows four to six in the space following.*

mute    swan

whistling    swan

trumpeter    swan

*How does the swan's long neck help him? Answer below in cursive.*

51

## Aim of the Lesson

To review the formation of the capital and small letters *U, V,* and *W* in slant print.

## Drill

Drill the children on the down, backward-slanting, and forward-slanting lines of slant print. Each should be practiced several times.

70

## Conducting the Class

1. Review the stroke formations of these six letter forms on the blackboard. (See number 1 below.) Notice that each small letter (with the exception of the letter *u*) is formed the same as its capital.

2. Have the children practice these forms in the air several times each.

3. Go over "Reminders" and have the children proceed with the lesson.

## Other Comments

1. The stroke formations for these letters are as follows:
    *U*—down, curve, up
    *u*— down, curve, up, down
    *V*—b-s line, f-s line
    *v*—b-s line, f-s line
    *W*—b-s line, f-s line, b-s line, f-s line
    *w*—b-s line, f-s line, b-s line, f-s line

2. Emphasize consistency of letter formation in this lesson. Encourage the children to make each letter right and to make every other letter like it. All *u*'s should look the same, all *w*'s should look the same, and so forth.

3. The answer to the question on line seven is: It helps him get his food.

# Lesson 25
# Small Cursive *o* and *c*

**Lesson 25  Small Cursive** *o* **and** *c*

Reminders:
  Be sure the letters in the sentence are spaced
the right distance apart.
  Be sure all your letters are slanted the same.

Most of us are familiar with the common crow—a large, shiny black bird with a loud caw. Farmers often do not like them, because they love to walk through a newly planted field and pick out all the seeds they can find! But they do eat many harmful bugs and worms that could hurt the farmers' crops.

*Trace the letters o and c, and copy them in the space following.*

*Copy the following sentence.*

Some crows can learn to talk.

*Copy the letters below in the space following.*

*a*                                         *d*

*What good thing do crows do for the farmer? Answer below.*

53

## Aim of the Lesson

To teach the children how to form the small cursive letters *o* and *c*.

## Drill

The children should practice the double-overcurve combination in the first two strokes of the letter *c* ( ). The overcurve-oval combination of the letter o begins similarly but continues around, forming a complete oval. Help the children make smooth, even strokes.

72

## Conducting the Class

1. Explain and demonstrate the stroke formations of these two letters on the blackboard.

2. Have the children practice the letters in the air in order to get the feel of making them.

3. The children should proceed with the lesson according to the directions.

## Other Comments

1. The stroke formations for these cursive letters are as follows:

   *o* —overcurve, oval, undercurve

   *c* —overcurve, overcurve, undercurve

2. Because these letters do not contain any slant lines at all, the children could have some difficulty in maintaining good form for them. A letter without any straight lines contributes to poor form.

3. Be sure the oval of the letter *o* has proper slant as well as proper width. It is also important that the oval be closed at the top.

4. With the letter *c*, the children should be able to see that there is a difference between the curvature of the first two strokes, though they are both overcurves. The second overcurve is more sharply curved than the first one.

5. It may be a little difficult to properly join the second overcurve with the final undercurve ( *c* ). The joining point should not really be sharp, but neither should it be totally rounded. The junction point should be noticeable. It will help the children to make a proper junction if they make the second overcurve back far enough. Also, the second overcurve should come almost to the bottom line before the undercurve begins.

6. The answer to the question of line seven is: They eat harmful bugs and worms.

## Practice Sentences

1. An albatross may follow a ship for days.
2. Crows like to live in open areas.
3. Crows eat the eggs of other birds.

# Lesson 26
# Small Cursive *m* and *n*

**Lesson 26  Small Cursive *m* and *n***

Reminders:
  Be sure you make each slant line of *m* and *n*
the same slant.
  Are you sitting up straight?

Magpies are large, black-and-white birds,
whose tails are longer than their bodies. They
are mainly to be found in the dry, open areas
of western North America. These birds are
very loud, noisy, and bold. To watch them fly
across the road in front of you with their long,
streaming tails is a beautiful sight.

*Trace the strokes, and copy the letters in rows one to three.*

*r n n m m m m*

*r n n m m m*

*Copy the following sentence.*

*Magpies will eat almost anything.*

*Copy these letters in the space following.*

*n*        *r*

*Which is longer—the tail or the body of a magpie? Answer below in a sentence.*

55

## Aim of the Lesson

To teach the children how to form the cursive small letters *m* and *n*.

## Drill

Have the children make long rows of overcurves and slants on the
blackboard ( *mm*, etc.). Have them try to make all of the humps as
nearly the same as possible.

74

## Conducting the Class

1. Show the children that both the letters *m* and *n* are made up primarily of overcurves and slants like the ones they practiced on the blackboard. Each letter, however, has a finishing undercurve stroke.

2. Following your explanation and demonstration of *m* and *n,* the children should practice them in the air several times.

3. Go over "Reminders" and have the children proceed with the lesson according to the directions.

## Other Comments

1. The stroke formations for the cursive letters *m* and *n* are as follows:

    *m*—overcurve, slant, overcurve, slant, overcurve, slant, under-curve

    *n*— overcurve, slant, overcurve, slant, undercurve

2. Emphasize the importance of good alignment with these letters, and especially in the sentence.

3. Emphasize proper joining of overcurves and slants. The junction point should be somewhat rounded, but not so round that you cannot recognize where the junction is. Help the children strike a balance between the extremes.

4. Check to be sure the children's movements are smooth-flowing, not stiff and jerky.

5. The answer to the question of line seven is: The tail is longer.

# Lesson 27

# *X, Y,* and *Z* in Slant Print

**Lesson 27** *X, Y,* and *Z* in Slant Print

Reminder:
  Be sure you have the proper slant on backward-slanting and forward-slanting lines.

The mockingbird is a famous imitator. That means he can sing the songs of other birds almost as well as they can! We might say he is a copycat. The mockingbird will often repeat many different bird songs in just a few minutes.

*Copy these letters in the space following.*

X                                        x

Y                                        y

Z                                        z

*Copy the following sentence.*

The mockingbird's color is gray.

*Copy these strokes in the space following.*

*Why can mockingbirds copy other birds' songs? Answer below in cursive.*

57

## Aim of the Lesson

To review the formation of the capital and small letters *X, Y,* and *Z* in slant print.

## Drill

Have the children practice the backward-slanting, forward-slanting, and across lines several times each.

## Conducting the Class

1. Review with the children the stroke formations of both the small and capital letters *X, Y,* and *Z*. Have them notice similarities and differences between the different forms.

2. The children should practice each form in the air several times.

3. Go over the "Reminder" and have the children proceed with the lesson.

## Other Comments

1. The stroke formations for these slant-print letters are as follows:

*X*— f-s line, b-s line

*x*— f-s line, b-s line

*Y*—b-s line, f-s line, down

*y*—b-s line, f-s line

*Z*—across, f-s line, across

*z*—across, f-s line, across

2. The answer to the question of line seven is: God made them that way.

3. Be sure the children make the two strokes of the letter *x* cross exactly in the middle of the space.

4. The letter *z* should make a perfect parallelogram ( ) when lines are drawn down each side, touching both points. Check the children's *z*'s. If they are not parallelograms, then they are not being made accurately.

5. In the sixth line the children are to make undercurves and overcurves, retracing each one up and down six or eight times.

## Practice Sentences

1. Sometimes mockingbirds damage fruit crops.
2. Magpies can be attracted to things that glitter.
3. Sometimes magpies become almost tame.

# Lesson 28
# Small Cursive *p* and *t*

**Lesson 28  Small Cursive** *p* **and** *t*

Reminders:
  Remember: *p* and *t* are not three lines high,
only two lines.
  Be careful to make your *p*'s and *t*'s the same
slant.

You may never have heard such strange
names as pipit and wagtail. But the birds with
these names are not so strange. The pipit is a
sparrow-sized, brownish bird which says its
own name. The wagtail has a bright yellow
breast and is in the same family as the pipit.

*Copy p̸ and ℒ in the space that follows them.*

ʲ ∱ ∱ p̸ p̸

∂ ∦ ∦ t

*Copy the words in this row in the row below.*

*pipit*    *pipit*    *pipit*    *pipit*    *pipit*    *pipit*

*Copy these letters in the space following.*

*m*                          *n*

*The wagtail's name describes a habit of both wagtails and pipits. What do you think this is?*

59

## Aim of the Lesson

To teach the children to form the cursive small letters *p* and *t*
properly.

## Drill

Have the children practice the undercurve-slant combination as
found in *p* and *t*.

78

## Conducting the Class

1. Demonstrate on the blackboard the formation of the cursive small letters *p* and *t*. Explain the stroke formations and point out the stroke similarities between the two letters.

2. The children should practice these letters in the air or on the blackboard if possible.

3. After going over "Reminders" with them and checking on posture, have the children proceed with the lesson according to the directions.

## Other Comments

1. The stroke formations for the cursive small letters *p* and *t* are as follows:

*p* —undercurve, slant, retrace, oval, undercurve

*t* —undercurve, slant, undercurve, across line (from slant manuscript)

2. The answer to the question in line seven is: They constantly bob (or wag) their tails.

3. Be sure the children make the letter *p* go up two spaces, not just one. They may have seen others write a short *p* and think that is the way to form it.

4. Be sure the cross on the letter *t* is at the right place up and down and is balanced from side to side. Also be sure it is straight across and not slanted.

5. Check the writing habits of your left-handed students. Are they writing smoothly and easily in the proper manner?

# Lesson 29
# Small Cursive *r* and *s*

**Lesson 29 Small Cursive** *r* **and** *s*

Reminder:
   Remember to make *r* and *s* just a little taller than the rest of the short letters.

Upon first thought, a sparrow might seem so common as to be uninteresting. But did you know that there are at least thirty-three different kinds of sparrows in North America alone, and many others in other parts of the world? One of the more common sparrows is the song sparrow. His song is a beautiful one, even though he is just a small, white-and-brown-striped bird.

*Copy these letters in the space following.*

*↲ ↳ ↳ ↳*

*↲ ↳ ↳*

*Copy this sentence in the line below.*

*Sparrows can be found almost everywhere.*

*Copy these letters in the space following.*

*t*                         *p*

*Do you know the names of any other sparrows? Write them below.*

61

## Aim of the Lesson

To teach the children to form the cursive small letters *r* and *s* accurately and neatly.

## Drill

Have the children practice the undercurve-undercurve combination as found in the first two strokes of the letter *r*.

## Conducting the Class

1. Explain and demonstrate the formation of the cursive small letters *r* and *s*. Explain that *r* and *s* are different from the rest of the cursive small letters in that neither of them touches a line exactly at the top. Both letters have points that come up a short distance above the first line.

2. Have the children practice these two letters in the air or on the blackboard several times to get the feel of them.

3. Following practice, go over the "Reminder" and have the children proceed with the lesson according to the directions.

## Other Comments

1. The stroke combinations for the cursive small letters *r* and *s* are as follows:

    *r* —undercurve, undercurve, slant, undercurve
    *s* —undercurve, undercurve, undercurve

2. Some answers to the question of line seven could be: chipping, English, tree, golden-crowned, or song sparrow. Use a bird book if you are uncertain about any of the children's answers. Help the children think of some if they cannot think of them on their own.

3. Be sure none of the children develop the habit of making the letter *r* in a sloppy fashion like any of these ( **ʌʌʃ** ), even though it is commonly made in these ways. The standard way to make this letter is with an undercurve, undercurve, slant, and undercurve.

4. Explain the difference in slant, length, and form of the three undercurves in the letter *s*. The first and last curves are quite regular, but the second curve is a little different. It has a touch of the double curve at the top, and curves very sharply near the bottom line. Help the children do a neat job at making this letter.

## Practice Sentences

1. The pipit dips up and down in flight.
2. Pipits have thin, sharp bills.
3. Sparrows have short, seed-cracking bills.

# Lesson 30
# Small Cursive Review

**Lesson 30  Small Cursive Review**

Reminders:
1. Remember to watch your posture. Are you sitting straight?
2. Are you holding your pencil gently and correctly?
3. Is your paper slanted at a proper angle?
4. Does each letter have the right slant?

5. Are your letters even across the top?
6. Do your letters touch the bottom line?
7. Is each letter the proper height?
8. Are you forming each letter as you learned it?

*Copy each letter in the space following.*

| *a* | *b* | *c* | *d* |
| *e* | *f* | *g* | *h* |
| *i* | *j* | *k* | *l* |
| *m* | *n* | *o* | *p* |
| *q* | *r* | *s* | *t* |
| *u* | *v* | *w* | *x* |
| *y* | *z* | | |

63

## Aim of the Lesson

To review every small letter of the cursive alphabet.

## Drill

Have the children say the names of the strokes of cursive writing and copy several of each on the blackboard or on other paper.

## Conducting the Class

Before the children begin this lesson, call their attention to the "Reminders" at the top of the page. Bring out each reminder forcefully. The first three are important to remember before beginning the lesson and are related to posture, pencil holding, and paper placement. The last five are related to the quality and form of the letters. The children should remind themselves of them as they write.

Have the children carefully proceed with the lesson according to the directions, copying each letter at least twice.

## Other Comments

1. If you know that the children are making any of the letters unsatisfactorily, be sure to have them practice until you are reasonably satisfied before they proceed beyond this point. Using several class periods if necessary in giving remedial help would be well worth the effort.

2. Carefully evaluate the children's work on these points, counting the following percents of the total grade for each item:
    a.  line quality (too light or too heavy)—10 percent
    b.  even alignment—20 percent
    c.  correct and consistent slant—20 percent
    d.  proper letter formation according to stroke—40 percent
    e.  evenness of movement (smoothly made lines)—10 percent

# Unit 2

# Cursive Capitals
# and
# Writing Quality

### Lessons 31–60

# Introduction to Unit 2

You may have been too busily engrossed over the past months, teaching the individual forms of the small cursive letters to notice how much your students have progressed in their general handwriting ability. Before you move into the next unit and introduce the capital letters, you should discern this by asking yourself a few questions.

First, consider your students' penmanship on papers in other subjects. Is it any poorer there than in penmanship class? It will take a lot of effort to get the same quality penmanship at other times as in penmanship class, but that is what learning penmanship is all about.

Do your children have a sense of what is proper posture, paper placement, and pencil holding, and assume that position automatically without always needing to be reminded?

Have your children caught the rhythmical feel of making the cursive letters? You should be able to see some of it in their writing. Continue to work on it throughout the rest of the year along with your teaching of capital letters. Compare their current writing (now and later) with earlier samples to see just how they are doing.

Do not succumb to the idea that it is not as important to learn capital letters well as it is to learn the small letters. True, they are not used as often, but an illegible capital letter can often be more difficult to decipher than a small letter poorly written. So be sure that the children learn them well.

Capital letters are somewhat more complex than small letters. The groundwork that has been laid in working with small letters will be an important help when it comes to learning the more detailed movements of capital letters.

Continue to make a strong secondary emphasis on writing quality, although learning the form of the letters should take the predominant place.

# Lesson 31
# Stroke Review
# and Introduction to Capitals

**Lesson 31  Stroke Review
                and Introduction to Capitals**

Reminder:
   Remember to sit straight, slant your paper correctly,
and hold your pencil in the proper way.

*Copy each stroke in the space following.*

*O*

*/*

*/*

*/*

*ſ*

*/*

*Copy these words in the space following.*

*learn  capital  letters*

67

## Aim of the Lesson

To review the basic cursive strokes, and to introduce the children to some general principles as related to the formation of cursive capital letters.

## Conducting the Class

1.  Have the children turn to the inside back cover, where the cursive capital letters are given. Introduce them again to capital letters,

and mention some principles related to their formation:

    a. All capital letters are full height—that is, they all go up three spaces.

    b. Many capital letters use the loop, and none of the small letters do.

    c. All capital letters are made from the six basic strokes, the same as small letters are.

    d. Most of the strokes of the capital letters are more complicated than the small letters. Demonstrate. Be quick to explain, however, that if the children follow the rules, the letters will not be hard to make well.

  2. Have them quickly practice the six strokes in the air.

  3. Go over "Reminder" and have the children proceed with the lesson.

## Other Comments

1. Be sure that the children make the loop as accurately as possible, since this is one stroke that they have not practiced much. Be sure the other strokes are made accurately and smoothly too.

2. In the last line, watch for proper letter spacing and correct joining of one letter to another.

## Practice Sentences

  1. Jesus is the Son of God.

  2. Jesus came down to earth.

  3. Jesus lived and died for us.

# Lesson 32
# Using Cursive Strokes
# to Make Capital Letters

**Lesson 32  Using Cursive Strokes**
              **to Make Capital Letters**

Reminder:
   Make each letter carefully according to the
example, and stroke by stroke.

*Fill each line with copies of the letters.*

*Copy one time in the space following.*

69

## Aim of the Lesson

To help the children see that cursive capital letters are composed of strokes similar to the strokes that make up small letters.

## Conducting the Class

1. Show the children the miscellaneous strokes at the beginning of each line. See if they can guess what the various strokes are. The children may be a little confused because some of the strokes may not

look exactly the same as they do when formed in the standard way.

2. Explain that these strokes are the individual strokes in the order that they appear in each letter that follows. To make each letter, the strokes must be put together in the right way.

3. Demonstrate on the blackboard how the strokes are put together to make each of these six letters. Explain carefully that all capital letters are made this same way from different combinations of the basic strokes.

4. After going over "Reminder," explain to the children that these letters will be learned more thoroughly later. Then have them proceed with the lesson.

## Other Comments

1. Following are the stroke combinations for each letter in this lesson:

   $\mathcal{N}$ —loop, slant, overcurve, slant, undercurve

   $\mathcal{S}$ — undercurve, double curve, undercurve

   $\mathcal{O}$ —large oval, undercurve

   $\mathcal{H}$ —loop, slant, overcurve, slant, overcurve, undercurve

   $\mathcal{B}$ —undercurve, slant, overcurve, undercurve, undercurve, undercurve

   $\mathcal{I}$ —overcurve, undercurve, undercurve

2. Do not expect perfection in this lesson in the making of these letters. That will be worked at more in the detailed lessons that follow. This lesson is primarily to show the relationship of individual strokes to the finished letter and to get the children in the habit of making proper capitals.

# Lesson 33
# Cursive Capitals *A* and *O*

**Lesson 33 Cursive Capitals** *A* **and** *O*

Reminders:
Remember to keep the slant line of the capital
*A* straight.
Remember to make the large oval smoothly
and neatly.

Auks are queer birds in the penguin family
that live in the North. Though much smaller
than penguins, they look like them in many
ways.
Owls are birds that have large heads and
short necks. Few people see them because they
usually come out only at night to hunt for small
animals.

*Copy the capital A in rows one and two.*

$\mathcal{A}\ \mathcal{A}\ \mathcal{A}$

*Copy each word in the space following.*

$\mathcal{A}uk$  $\mathcal{A}ll$  $\mathcal{A}ny$

*Copy the capital O in rows four and five.*

$\mathcal{O}\ \mathcal{O}$

*Copy each word in the space following.*

$\mathcal{O}wl$  $\mathcal{O}at$  $\mathcal{O}live$

*Copy these letters in the space that follows.*

$a$  $o$

71

## Aim of the Lesson

To teach the children to make the cursive capital letters *A* and *O*
neatly and accurately.

## Drill

Have the children practice the large oval several times.

92

## Conducting the Class

1.  Explain and demonstrate the formation of the letters *A* and *O*. Show that these two letters are both based on the large oval. The oval of the letter *A* is slightly flatter than the oval of the letter *O* and has a little corner at the top.

2.  Following your explanations and demonstrations, the children should practice each letter a number of times in the air or on the blackboard.

3.  Go over "Reminders" and the directions with the children. Then have them proceed to do the lesson as you supervise each child's work carefully.

## Other Comments

1.  Following are the stroke combinations for the capital letters *A* and *O:*

    $\mathcal{A}$ —oval, slant, undercurve

    $\mathcal{O}$ —large oval, undercurve

2.  Be sure the children slant their ovals sufficiently. There is a tendency for children of this age to make their ovals too large and round. As a result they lose their slant. Guard against this.

3.  The oval on *A* should be squashed and slanted enough to leave a sizable space at the bottom between the oval and the slant.

## Practice Sentences

1.  Auks can swim underwater, using their wings.
2.  Auks are colored black and white.
3.  Owls can fly swiftly and silently.

# Lesson 34
# Cursive Capital *C*

**Lesson 34  Cursive Capital** *C*

Reminder:
  Be sure your paper is slanted properly so
that your letters have the right form.

The cormorant is a blackish-looking water
bird. It can be found both inland around lakes
and rivers, and along the seashore. One of its
main foods is fish, which it dives underwater
to catch.

*Trace each backward loop, and copy it in the space that follows.*

*Trace the letter* C, *and copy it in rows two and three.*

*Copy the following sentence twice.*

*Cormorants fly in flocks like geese.*

*Copy these letters in the space that follows.*

73

## Aim of the Lesson

To teach the children to form the cursive capital letter *C* correctly.

## Drill

Have the children practice the overcurve and undercurve combination as in the two final strokes of the letter C ( $\mathcal{C}$ ).

## Conducting the Class

1. Explain and demonstrate on the blackboard the proper formation of the letter *C*. Explain that the letter *C* is made entirely of curves, with no straight lines anywhere in the letter. It is based on the large oval, though it is not a complete oval itself. So we separate it into several smaller strokes. Capital *C* is unusual in that it begins with a backward loop. Among the other capitals, only the letter *E* begins in the same way.

2. Following your explanation and demonstration, have the children practice the letter several times in the air.

3. Go over "Reminder" and the directions; then have the children proceed with the lesson under your supervision. Be sure to give them correction where it is needed.

## Other Comments

1. The stroke combination for the letter C is as follows:

    *C* —loop, overcurve, undercurve

2. Be sure the children make the backward loop properly; this is one of the more difficult strokes. One thing that may help is giving specific instructions to the children as to where the loop begins, how far down it comes before going up again, and the general slant of the loop. Careful demonstration will also help to prevent confusion. Be sure the children's loops close at the top.

3. The children should also join the overcurve and undercurve accurately. The point of joining should be definitely noticeable. Call the children's attention to the fact that just above the bottom line the curve is sharper. That is where the overcurve and undercurve join, and that point should be seen in all the children's letter *C*'s. Showing a clear overcurve and undercurve gives the letter shape, form, and slant. The letter should look like this ( *C* ), not like this ( **C** ).

4. All in all, the children's letter *C*'s should have about the same width as a properly formed oval. The tendency of some children will be to make a big, wide letter ( **C** ), and of others to make it too narrow ( *C* ).

# Lesson 35
# Cursive Capitals *I* and *J*

**Lesson 35  Cursive Capitals** *I* **and** *J*

Reminders:
  Remember to rest each letter firmly on the bottom line.
  Remember to make all the strokes of the letter *J* cross exactly at the bottom line.

The ibis is a strange-looking bird that lives mostly in marshes along the coast. It has a very long and beautifully curved bill and is in the heron family.
  Jaegers look much like gulls, but you will find them only in the far North or over the ocean. They eat fish and small animals, while gulls eat mostly dead things.

*Copy the capital I in rows one and two.*

*I I*

*Copy each word in the space following.*

*Ibis*          *It*          *I'll*

*Copy the capital J in rows four and five.*

*J J*

*Copy each word in the space following.*

*Jaeger*          *Jesus*

*Copy these letters in the space that follows.*

*C*          *i*          *j*

75

## Aim of the Lesson

To teach the children to form the cursive capital letters *I* and *J* accurately and neatly.

## Drill

The children should practice the overcurve as it is in the beginning stroke of each of these letters.

96

## Conducting the Class

1.  Demonstrate and explain the formation of each of these letters: first *I,* and then *J.* Explain that these letters stand in a class separate from the other capitals because they both begin with an overcurve. The overcurve of the letter *I* begins at the bottom line, whereas the overcurve of the letter *J* starts below the bottom line. From the top, the second stroke of the letter *I* curves down to the bottom line and back up in one long, backward undercurve. The second stroke of the letter *J* goes straight down to 1½ spaces below the bottom line. Capital *I* finishes off with an undercurve, and capital *J* with an overcurve.

2.  The children should practice each of these letters a few times in the air, following your explanation.

3.  Go over "Reminders" and the directions; then have the children proceed with the lesson.

## Other Comments

1.  The stroke combinations for the two letters of this lesson are:

    *I* —overcurve, undercurve, undercurve

    *J* —overcurve, slant, overcurve

2.  Help the children to get the initial overcurve of each of these two letters properly slanted so that the rest of the letter turns out right. The finished overcurve should have the same basic angle as a slant line. In other words, it should be almost vertical, but leaning a little to the right.

3.  The first undercurve of the letter *I* is critical to its proper formation. The children should curve it gently until it gets near the bottom line and then curve it more sharply the rest of the way. It should touch the first line up from the bottom, and then the letter finishes with a final, short undercurve.

4.  The children should be careful to make the back of the letter *J* as perfectly straight as possible from top to bottom.

## Practice Sentences

1.  Cormorants often perch with their wings partly opened.
2.  Ibises fly by flapping their wings and then gliding.
3.  Jaegers fly with sharply bent wings.

# Lesson 36

# Size

**Lesson 36  Size**

Reminder:
  Remember to form the letters correctly, even though you are thinking mostly about their size.

You should pay careful attention to the size of your writing. The dotted lines in your penmanship book help you to make your letters the right size when you do your penmanship lesson. You want to be sure your writing is the right size even when there are no light gray lines to follow.

Writing that is too small strains the eyes of the one reading it. Writing that is too large wastes space and can be hard to read because it makes the lines run together. We should be kind to those who read our writing by making our letters the right size.

*This writing is too large. This is too*

*small. This writing is just right.*

Can you write these words the right size even without guidelines (twice on guidelines, twice on base line only)?

*write*

*letters*

*right*

*size*

Copy these letters in the space following.

*I*                    *J*

77

## Aim of the Lesson

To teach the children what correct size is and how to make their letters that size.

## Drill

The children should practice multiple "ups and downs" for review, either in the air or on the blackboard.

## Conducting the Class

1. Before discussing the reasons for writing the correct size that are given at the top of the page, ask the children to give you some reasons why our writing should not be either too large or too small. Explain that crowded, tiny writing or cluttered, oversize writing is unpleasant to read.

2. Demonstrate on the blackboard what happens when writing is too large (the lines of writing run into each other).

3. Demonstrate writing that is too small. Show how difficult it is to read. It will mean more if you demonstrate it than if they just see it in the book.

4. After going over "Reminder" and the directions with the children, have them proceed with the lesson accordingly.

## Other Comments

1. The real test of size is the child's writing in his daily work. Next best is his writing in penmanship class without guidelines to regulate the size and alignment. So pay special attention to the words written without guidelines when it comes to evaluation of this lesson.

2. Do not make proportion (that is, the height relationship of different letters and parts of letters) an important part of this lesson. This will be emphasized in Lesson 37.

3. It would be well for you to call attention to the importance of size consistency. The size of the letters should not vary much from one place to another, and the size of each word should be the same as that of each other word.

4. Some questions to ask about the size of the children's handwriting:
   a. Are the small letters too small?
   b. Is the last letter in each word large enough? (There is a tendency to decrease size toward the end of a word, especially the size of the last letter.)

# Lesson 37
# Proportion

**Lesson 37  Proportion**

Reminders:
  Remember to rest each letter firmly on the bottom line, not above or below.
  Be sure you make each letter correctly.

Proportion means how high one letter or part of a letter is compared to another. Letters are of three heights. The small letters are the shortest. Medium letters like *t* and *d* are twice as high. Full-height or tall letters are three times as high as small letters.

Your lessons have had light gray lines to help you make each letter and portion of each letter the correct height. Can you keep each letter the correct height even when there are no light gray lines to guide you?

Here is the proper height of each letter: full height— *b, f, h, k, l,* all capitals
medium— *d, p, t*
small— *a, c, e, g, i, j, m, n, o, q, r, s, u, v, w, x, y, z*

*This writing does not have good proportion.*

*This writing has correct proportion.*

Write these words three times each, once with light gray lines, twice without.

*make*

*letters*

*right*

*proportion*

Write "*God is pleased with good work*" on the line below.

## Aim of the Lesson

To help the children learn the height relationships between various letters and parts of letters.

## Drill

Have the children warm up by practicing multiple ovals.

## Conducting the Class

1. Explain that, along with writing words the proper size, it is important that we write letters the correct height in relation to other letters. That is what this lesson is about.

2. Go over the paragraphs at the top of the lesson. Demonstrate correct and incorrect proportion on the blackboard. Call careful attention to which letters are three lines high, which are two, and which are one.

3. After you have explained the directions and have gone over "Reminders," the children should proceed with the lesson. Be sure to maintain constant supervision of your pupils' work to ensure proper size, proportion, and letter formation.

## Other Comments

1. It would be well to briefly mention the fact that the downward loops also have proportion. They should end approximately 1½ spaces below the baseline.

2. Call attention to the *parts* of letters that relate to proper proportion, such as the lower parts of *h* and *k*.

3. It seems to be quite easy for children to forget that t and d are only two spaces high, not three, or that the full-height letters are three spaces high, not two. Frequently one sees *t*'s and *d*'s the same height as the full-height letters, and the full-height letters only twice as high as the small letters. Work hard to curb this tendency now, before it becomes a habit.

4. Again, make your primary evaluation of the children's work on their writing where there are no lines to guide size and proportion. Grade for size as well as proportion.

## Practice Sentences

1. God expects us to do our best.
2. Carelessness has no place.
3. We want to write as well as we can.

# Lesson 38
# Cursive Capital *L*

**Lesson 38  Cursive Capital** *L*

Reminders:
  Make the double curves of the letter *L* smooth and even.
  Be sure to make the letter *L* about the same slant as the other letters.

Longspurs live mostly in dry, open areas with few trees. They are much like sparrows with short, heavy bills. God has made them this way so that they can crack and eat seeds. Sparrows usually like to live in areas with more trees than longspurs do.

*Copy the stroke combinations in the space that follows.*

*Copy the letter* $\mathcal{L}$ *in rows two to four.*

*Copy the following sentence in row six.*

Longspurs  walk,  but  seldom  hop.

*Write the letter* $\mathcal{L}$ *three times. Then write the words* Longspurs, walk, *and* seldom.

L.F. 50
St. 15
Pr. 15
G.N. 20
Total

81

## Aim of the Lesson

To teach the children the accurate and smooth formation of the cursive capital letter *L*.

## Drill

Have the children practice double curves.

102

## Conducting the Class

1. Following drill, explain to the children that the letter *L* has two sets of double curves. It is therefore important that they learn to make a smooth and even double curve.

2. Demonstrate, and explain while doing so, the formation of the capital letter *L*. Let the children see that this letter is nothing but a combination of graceful curves, with no straight lines at all.

3. The children should practice the letter *L* several times in the air.

4. After you have gone over "Reminders" and the directions, have the children proceed with the lesson as you supervise their work.

## Other Comments

1. The stroke combinations for the letter *L* are as follows:
   *ℒ* —undercurve, double curve, double curve

2. The letter *L* being one of those letters with no backbone of straight lines, you will need to take special effort to help the children give the letter good form. It is one of the most attractive letters if properly made.

3. The key to an attractive *L* is graceful double curves. They should be made like this ( ﹀ ), not like this ( ∿ ).

4. Notice that *L* begins at the halfway point, halfway between the first and second lines.

5. Be sure the loops of this letter are the proper size.

6. Do not encourage joining *L* to other letters. It can be done, but it detracts from the gracefulness of the writing.

7. Be sure the children put to practice what they have learned about size and proportion in the last two lessons.

8. An evaluation chart is being included in this lesson and will also be a part of lessons to follow. As we advance into new areas of quality study, other areas will be added to the evaluation chart.

**L.F.** means *letter formation*. Deduct from 1 to 50 points for improper formation, and write a number that you think accurately reflects the child's letter formation. If, for example, a child crossed his letter *t*'s at the wrong place, deduct 3 points from the total of 50 points for letter formation, or whatever amount you decide upon.

**Sz.** stands for *size*. Deduct for incorrect size, either too large or too small.

**Pr.** stands for *proportion*. Deduct for in accurate proportion.

**G.N.** stands for *general neatness.* Deduct for eraser smudges, sloppiness, and carelessness.

When finished with the evaluation (evaluate only the last line), add the numbers together. The answer is the grade for that lesson. Following is a sample:

| | | |
|------|------|------|
| **L.F.** | 50 | 45 |
| **Sz.** | 15 | 13 |
| **Pr.** | 15 | 15 |
| **G.N.** | 20 | 19 |
| | **Total** | 92% |

# Lesson 39
# Cursive Capital *B*

**Lesson 39  Cursive Capital** *B*

Reminders:
  Remember to make your curves as smooth and even as possible.
  Make the "backs" of the letter *B* all have the same slant.

Bluebirds are not the only blue birds, but the males do have beautiful blue backs and orange breasts. You would look for them in orchards and farmyards. They are very helpful birds because they eat annoying insects, helping to keep them in control.

*Copy these stroke combinations in the spaces following.*

*3*                                          *3*

*Trace the strokes; then copy the letter* ℬ *in rows two and three.*

*1 1 P ℬ ℬ*

*Copy this sentence in row five.*

*Berries are in the bluebird's diet.*

*Copy the letter* ℒ *in the space following.*

*ℒ*

*Copy these words on the following line:* *Berries, in, bluebird's, diet*

L.P.  50
St.   15
Pr.   15
G.N.  20
Total

83

## Aim of the Lesson

To teach the children to make the cursive capital letter *B* accurately.

## Drill

The children should practice tall undercurve-slant-overcurve combinations as drill.

## Conducting the Class

1. Explain to the children the formation of the letter $B$ and demonstrate it stroke by stroke. (Be sure you can make it well before trying to demonstrate it.) Show the children that two other letters begin the same way, the letters $P$ and $R$. These three letters all begin with an undercurve, slant, and overcurve.

2. Following explanation and demonstration, the children should practice writing the letter several times before doing the lesson.

3. After going over "Reminders" and the directions, have the children proceed with the lesson.

## Other Comments

1. The stroke combinations for the letter $B$ are as follows:
   $\mathcal{B}$ —undercurve, slant, overcurve, undercurve, undercurve, undercurve

2. The critical part of the letter $B$ is in getting the curves properly made. The upper part and the lower part should be the same size, and in line with each other on approximately the same slant as the slant line ( $\mathcal{B}$ ). Both curves should be made smoothly. Both curves should extend forward from the slant line the same distance. Also be sure the letter does not get too wide or too narrow.

3. You will want to be sure that the next-to-last stroke touches the slant line, and at a point just above the bottom line.

4. In teaching all the cursive capitals, point out just where the first stroke begins, where the loops close or touch, which parts should be aligned, and so forth. Many errors in formation are simply the result of poor observation.

5. Somewhere about this time you should be paying increased attention to the rate of writing of each child. Be sure he is not spending long periods of time "drawing" the letters to perfection. The writing should keep moving across the page with an even motion.

## Practice Sentences

1. Mountain bluebirds are blue all over.
2. We are glad God put beauty in nature.
3. God can make our lives beautiful too.

# Lesson 40
# Cursive Capitals *P* and *R*

**Lesson 40  Cursive Capitals *P* and *R***

Reminders:
Remember to hold your pencil loosely and with fingers stretched out.
Be sure to make the third stroke of these letters very smoothly.

Pelicans are very large, odd-looking birds that live by fishing. They scoop up the fish in their large throat pouches.
Redpolls are small northern birds that can easily be recognized by a bright red patch on their foreheads. They eat many weed seeds.

*Copy the letters P and R in the rows following each letter.*

*Copy each letter in the space following.*

*Copy each word in the space following.*

Pelican          Put          Pull

Redpoll          Rope

85

## Aim of the Lesson

To teach the children to make the cursive capital letters *P* and *R* correctly.

## Drill

Have the children write the word *pull* several times in cursive as you say the strokes (first demonstrate on the board):

*pull*—under, slant, retrace, oval under, slant, under, slant under, slant, under, slant, under

107

## Conducting the Class

1. Following drill, demonstrate and explain the formation of the letters $P$ and $R$. Show the resemblance of these letters to the letter $B$ in the first four strokes. Also emphasize the difference between $P$ and $R$.

2. After you have given a good demonstration, the children should practice making these two letters in the air stroke by stroke as you call them out.

3. Once the children have practiced and you have looked together at "Reminders" and the directions for the lesson, have them proceed with the lesson.

## Other Comments

1. The stroke formations for these two letters are as follows:

   $P$ —undercurve, slant, overcurve, undercurve

   $R$ —undercurve, slant, overcurve, undercurve, overcurve, undercurve

2. The final overcurve-undercurve combination of the letter $R$ is not being called a double curve because it does not have the gracefulness of a properly made double curve. Take special pains that these two strokes are made according to pattern, with the overcurve quite sharp and the junction between the overcurve and undercurve also quite sharp.

3. Put strong emphasis on making the curves smoothly with both these letters.

4. Do not neglect to maintain a continual campaign against pencil pinching. Help the children maintain constant movement of the arm and an even rate of writing across the page. Rate and rhythm in writing can be helped by giving attention to activities like those in the drill section of this lesson.

5. Again, grade just the words written in the last two lines, paying special attention to the formation of the capital letters $P$ and $R$.

# Lesson 41
# Letter Spacing

**Lesson 41 Letter Spacing**

Reminders:
    Remember to put your book or paper on the proper slant.
    Remember to make each letter correctly.
    Remember to make your writing flow evenly and smoothly across the page.

It is important for us to learn to space our letters properly. This means having the right amount of distance between the letters.
    We should have all the letters in our words about the *same* distance apart. Our writing should not have some letters squeezed close together with others much farther apart.
    The letters should also be the *correct* distance apart, neither too crowded together nor too far apart. Either way makes the writing hard to read.

*This writing is not spaced right.*
Copy this sentence once in row three.

*This writing is spaced correctly.*

Copy this sentence in row five.

*Put proper distance between letters.*

Copy the letter *p* to the end of the row.

*p*

Copy each word in the space following.

L F   40
St.   10
Pr.   15
G N   15
L S   29
Total

*important*                    *idea*

87

## Aim of the Lesson

To teach the children the principles of letter spacing for cursive writing.

## Drill

Have the children write the word *letters* by strokes as you call them out. Increase speed each time you say the strokes. The strokes for this word are as follows: under, slant, under, (hook), slant, under, slant, under, slant, under, (hook), slant, under, under, slant, under, under, under, cross, cross.

## Conducting the Class

1. Go over the three paragraphs at the top of the page. Especially be sure the children are aware of the three kinds of incorrect spacing. If you have time, demonstrate each. If not, call attention to each kind of incorrect spacing in the first row.

2. Look at the second row with the children. They should be brought to admire the attractiveness of these properly spaced letters in comparison with the first row.

3. After you are sure the children have a clear understanding of letter spacing, go over "Reminders" and the directions. Then have the children proceed with the lesson under your supervision.

## Other Comments

1. The key to consistent and accurate spacing is a constant, even movement across the page. Assist the children in doing this.

2. Even though the emphasis is on spacing, be sure to insist that size, proportion, and letter formation continue to be accurate and correct in each child's work.

3. **L.S.** on the grading chart stands for *letter spacing*—an evaluation category that will continue from now on.

4. The children may soon catch on that only the last row is graded, and may then tend to get sloppy in the other rows of work. One way to take care of this is to deduct a certain amount from the final grade for obvious carelessness on any of the other rows also. They should do their best on all their work.

## Practice Sentences

1. Pelicans are very good flyers.
2. Brown pelicans can dive 30 feet* (9 meters) for fish.
3. Redpolls rise and fall when flying.

*Note:* The measurements in this course are given both in common and in metric units. For the practice sentences, you may wish to have your students write only the units with which they are most familiar.

# Lesson 42
# Word Spacing

**Lesson 42  Word Spacing**

Reminders:
Do not forget to space your letters correctly too.
Do not forget to keep your writing flowing smoothly across the page.

Proper spacing of words is just as important as proper spacing of letters within a word. The words in a sentence should not be too close together or too far apart.

The words we write should all be the same distance apart. We should leave about the width of one letter between words.

If our words are spaced too far apart, paper is wasted. If they are too close together, the writing is hard to read.

*These words          are          spaced incorrectly.*

*Copy this sentence in row three.*

*These  words  are  correctly  spaced.*

*Copy this sentence in row five.*

*Put  the  proper  distance  between  words.*

*Copy the letter R to the end of the row.*

*R*

*Copy this sentence in the space following.*

L.F. 40
Sz. 10
Pr. 10
G.N. 20
L.S. 10
W.S. 10
Total

*I  am  not  to  go.*

89

## Aim of the Lesson

To teach the children to space words properly in a sentence.

## Drill

Have the children write the word *correct* by strokes several times as you call out the strokes. The strokes are as follows: over, over, double, oval, under, under, slant, under, under, slant, under (hook), slant, double, over, under, slant, under, cross.

## Conducting the Class

1. Following drill, go over the paragraphs at the top of the lesson with the children. On the blackboard, demonstrate words that are too close together and words that are too far apart.

2. Look at the first line, showing improper spacing. Then contrast it with the second line. Be sure the children know just how far apart the words *are* to be spaced.

3. When you are sure the children understand how words are to be spaced, go over "Reminders" and the directions with them. Then have them proceed with the lesson.

## Other Comments

1. The key to consistent word spacing, like letter spacing, lies in maintaining a constant, even, and relaxed movement across the page, not windshield-wiper style movement at the wrist, but moving the entire forearm from the elbow.

2. As a guideline for spacing, tell the children that the space between words should be about the same as the width of one letter a.

3. **W.S.** on the grading scale stands for *word spacing*. Evaluate for correct word spacing in the children's work.

# Lesson 43
# Cursive Capital *S*

**Lesson 43  Cursive Capital** *S*

Reminders:
  Be sure you rest your letters squarely and
firmly on the bottom line.
  Remember to make each letter correctly.

Swifts are medium-sized, tube-shaped birds
that can easily be confused with swallows.
They live up to their name by being speedy
fliers. One kind of swift, called the chimney
swift, has the strange habit of resting and
nesting in tall chimneys.

*Copy this double curve in the space following.*

*Copy the letter* ∫ *in rows two and three.*

*Copy this sentence once in row five.*

Swifts can fly all day without resting.

*Copy the letter* ∠ *in the space following.*

*Write the letter* ∫ *three times. Then write the words* Swift, Songs, *and* Soft.

L F   40
St    10
Pr    10
G N   20
L S   10
W S   10
    ToGr

91

## Aim of the Lesson

To teach the children the proper formation of the cursive capital
letter *S*.

## Drill

Have the children write the word *swift* stroke by stroke as you call
out the strokes. The strokes are as follows: under, under, under, slant,
under, slant, under, retrace, under, slant, under, slant, under, under,

113

slant, under, dot, cross. Be sure the children are actually making the letters by strokes as you call them, not simply writing the word as they please.

## Conducting the Class

1. Demonstrate and explain the formation of the cursive letter *S*. This letter is all curves: two undercurves and a double curve. We want to make smooth, well-balanced curves so that our letter looks right.

2. The children should practice the letter *S* in the air several times.

3. After you go over "Reminders" and the directions with them, the children should proceed with the lesson.

## Other Comments

1. The stroke combination for the letter *S* is as follows:
*S* —undercurve, double curve, undercurve

2. It is important that the capital *S* has a proper slant and well-balanced formation. It should not be vertical ( ). If it is not slanted enough, it is also likely to be too broad.

3. Neither should the letter appear to be falling over backward ( ) or forward ( ) . Tell the children that the letter should not be nodding its head forward or backward, but it should be holding its head up straight.

## Practice Sentences

1. Swifts like flying insects for food.
2. Swifts are very swift.
3. Chimney swifts make their nests of twigs.

# Lesson 44
# Cursive Capital *G*

**Lesson 44  Cursive Capital** *G*

Reminders:
  Remember to make your curves smoothly.
  Be sure each letter touches the lines it
should and does not go above or below them.

Gnatcatchers are part of a warbler family,
most of which live in parts of the world outside
North America. They are small, blue-gray birds
with very thin insect-catching bills.

*Copy these two strokes in combination to the end of the row.*

ℓ

*Copy the capital letter 𝒢 in rows two and three.*

/  𝒫  𝒢  𝒢

*Copy the following sentence in row five.*

𝒢natcatchers really do eat gnats.

*Copy the letter g to the end of the row.*

g

L.F   45
No   10
Po   10
G.N   20
L.S   10
W.S   10
Total

*Copy the letter 𝒢 three times. Then write the words 𝒢ive, 𝒢o, and 𝒢ame*

## Aim of the Lesson

To teach the children to form the cursive capital letter *G* correctly.

## Drill

Start a series of drills on the basic strokes, beginning in this lesson with the undercurve. The children should practice the undercurve a number of times with the intent of improving the smoothness and evenness of the curve.

## Conducting the Class

1. Demonstrate and explain the formation of the cursive capital *G*. Explain that this letter is made of all undercurves, four of them, with two of the undercurves forming a loop between them. Also show the similarities between *G* and *S* by superimposing the letter *S* on the letter *G* ( *𝒮* ).

2. Have the children practice the letter *G* stroke by stroke in the air as you call the strokes out.

3. After you go over "Reminders" and the directions, have the children proceed with the lesson under your supervision.

## Other Comments

1. The stroke combination for the capital letter *G* is as follows:

   *𝒢*—undercurve, undercurve, undercurve, undercurve

2. Be sure the children understand that although this letter is all undercurves, the undercurves are not all alike. The third undercurve, in particular, is different. The middle of this curve is much sharper than either end. Help the children make each curve in this letter properly.

3. Like the letter *S,* this letter should have proper form. It should be slanted, not vertical. Above all, it should not be too wide, especially at the bottom. Few things look more ill-fitting in writing than a *G* that is too wide and flat ( *𝒢* ).

# Lesson 45
# Cursive Capitals *H* and *K*

**Lesson 45  Cursive Capitals *H* and *K***

Reminders:
   Remember to make each loop on both the letters *H* and *K* carefully.
   Be sure you make your curves smoothly and your slant lines straight.

Hummingbirds are the smallest of all North American birds. Their wings flap so rapidly that they produce a humming sound. They suck nectar from flowers for food.
   Killdeers have a habit of saying their name over and over again! You often see these brown-and-white birds with black breast bands fluttering over fields and pastures.

*Copy the capital and small letter H in the space that follows them.*

*ʃ 𝒥. 𝒥ℓ 𝓗 𝓗*

*h*

*Copy each word once in the space that follows.*

*Hummingbird*                     *Help*

*Copy the capital and small letter K in the space that follows them.*

*ʃ 𝒥. 𝒦 𝓚*

*k*

*Copy each word once in the space that follows it.*

*Killdeer*                     *Kindness*

L.F. 40
Sz. 10
Pr 10
G.N 20
L.S 10
W.S 10
Total

*Write the letters H and K twice each. Then write Heaven and Kneeling.*

95

## Aim of the Lesson

To teach the children to form the cursive capital letters *H* and *K* correctly.

## Drill

Have the children continue the drill series on the strokes—this time on the overcurve. Emphasize proper hand movement. Be sure they make this stroke smoothly and evenly.

117

## Conducting the Class

1. Demonstrate and explain the formation of the letters $H$ and $K$. Both are two-stage letters; the pencil has to be lifted and repositioned in the middle of making each one. Both letters begin with a loop-slant combination. Both begin the second stage at the same place and with an overcurve. The last several strokes are what make the two letters different from each other.

2. After your demonstration and explanation of these letters, have the children practice them in the air several times.

3. Go over "Reminders" and the directions. Then the children should proceed with the lesson under your supervision.

## Other Comments

1. The stroke formations for the letters $H$ and $K$ are as follows:

   $\mathcal{H}$ —loop, slant, overcurve, slant, overcurve, undercurve

   $\mathcal{K}$ —loop, slant, double curve, overcurve, undercurve

2. Work hard on proper formation of the loop. This is possibly the most difficult stroke of all to make correctly. It should be a smooth combination of a short undercurve and long overcurve. The overcurve should always close the figure with a gap. Following are some improper ways of forming the loop: ꟼ ℓ ℓ

3. It may be difficult for the children to properly match the two parts of these letters. This will come with practice. The two sides of the letter $H$ should be the right distance apart. The double curve of $K$ must start at the right place so that it will just be finished by the time it reaches the slant line. Watch the relationship between the two parts of these letters in the children's work.

4. You may wish to point out that the last two strokes of $K$ are much like those in $R$.

## Practice Sentences

1. All hummingbirds can fly backward.
2. Hummingbirds are sometimes quite fierce.
3. Killdeers are very noisy birds.

# Lesson 46
# Cursive Capitals *M* and *N*

## Aim of the Lesson

To teach the children to form the cursive letters *M* and *N* properly.

## Drill

In this lesson the children should practice the slant line. First have them make a few sets of multiple "ups and downs" and then individual slant lines. Be sure that the lines are straight, without waves or wiggles; that they begin and end at the right places; and that they all have correct and consistent slant.

## Conducting the Class

1. Explain and demonstrate the formation of the capital letters *M* and *N*. Show that the relationship between the capital letters *M* and *N* is much like that between the small letters *m* and *n*. The letter *M* always has one more hump than the letter *N*. The capitals each have one less hump respectively than the small letters.

2. After you have explained and demonstrated these letters, have the children practice each letter in the air several times before doing the lesson.

3. Go over "Reminder" and the directions, and then have them proceed with the lesson.

## Other Comments

1. The stroke formations for the letters *M* and *N* are as follows:
   *m* —loop, slant, overcurve, slant, overcurve, slant, undercurve
   *n* —loop, slant, overcurve, slant, undercurve

2. Be sure there is the proper degree of roundness at the junction of the overcurve and slant. The point should not be really sharp, but it should be definite and noticeable.

3. Pay special attention to the "Reminder" and emphasize it strongly.

4. Be sure the children are making their loops neatly and according to proper form.

# Lesson 47
# Slant (Part 1)

**Lesson 47 Slant** (Part 1)

*Slant* means how much a letter is leaning or if it is straight up and down. Correct slant leans forward a little from straight up and down. Notice how the writing in this lesson leans. You should try to make your writing lean about this much too.

Reminder:
While thinking about the slant of your writing, do not forget to watch other areas of handwriting too, like word and letter spacing, size, and proportion.

Every letter should have the same slant. One letter should not be slanted one way, and the next letter the other way.

*This writing is not properly slanted.*

Copy this sentence in the line below.

*This writing has the correct slant.*

Copy the sentence below in the next line.

*All letters should be slanted the same.*

Copy this letter to the end of the row.

*m*

L.F. 30
Sl. 10
Sc. 10
Pr. 10
G.N. 20
L.S. 10
W.S. 10
Total

On the line below write the sentence *"God will take care of you"* Be sure the slant is right.

99

## Aim of the Lesson

To make the children more aware of slant in writing, and to have them understand what correct slant is.

## Drill

Have the children drill on the oval stroke. You may want to tie it in with point number 2 under "Conducting the Class." Help the children to properly slant the oval.

## Conducting the Class

1. The important thing in this lesson is to go over the information in the upper right corner, emphasizing each principle for proper slant as given.

2. Before doing the lesson, the children should practice in the air handwriting movements with the proper slant.

3. Go over "Reminder" and the directions; then have the children proceed with the lesson while you supervise to be sure that they are slanting their letters properly.

## Other Comments

1. In this lesson, work primarily on creating an awareness of correct slant. In the next lesson the emphasis will be on ways to make it easy to slant letters correctly.

2. Slant lines form the backbone of correctly slanted handwriting. This is why you should emphasize that slant lines stay straight *from top to bottom* and do not *ever* curve.

3. **Sl.** on the grading scale stands for *slant,* of course. Deduct for inconsistent slant as well as for consistent but incorrect slant.

## Practice Sentences

1. Mergansers usually have white wing patches.
2. Males and females are colored differently.
3. The nutcracker nests near the timberline.

# Lesson 48
# Slant (Part 2)

**Lesson 48 Slant** (Part 2)

Reminders:
Do not fail to pay attention to your word and letter spacing.
Remember to hold your pencil loosely and with stretched-out fingers.

How can you make all your letters have the proper slant? One way is to be sure your paper is slanted properly. It will be hard to have correct slant if your paper is straight up and down on your desk.
Another way is to keep your hand moving across the page. Do not let it stop and rest at any spot for long. The slant will probably not be correct if you make your hand work like a windshield wiper.

*Copy this verse on the lines below it. (Matthew 6:26)*

"Behold the fowls of the air: for they sow not,

neither do they reap, nor gather into barns;

yet your heavenly Father feedeth them."

*Copy the letter n to the end of the row.*

n

101

## Aim of the Lesson

To teach the children the how of making properly slanted letters.

## Drill

The loop should come up for drill today. The children have been concentrating on the loop in past lessons, so it should not take much explanation. Emphasize smooth movement in making this stroke.

## Conducting the Class

1. Go over the points from the upper right corner of the workbook page carefully with the children.

2. Be sure all the children slant their papers correctly before doing the lesson.

3. Have the children practice keeping constant hand movement across the page. Do not let them write windshield-wiper style, that is, moving just the hand until they can reach no farther, then moving the arm, and repeating the process to the end of each line.

4. After going over "Reminders" and the directions, have the children proceed with the lesson.

## Other Comments

1. The hardest thing you will have to face in teaching the principles of this lesson is getting the children to maintain proper arm movement across the page. The principle is that the wrist joint, in general, should remain straight. The arm should pivot from the elbow, and the fingers should make the basic up and down strokes of the letters.

2. Combine form emphasis with movement emphasis. Whenever you emphasize either form or movement exclusively, the other one will suffer.

# Lesson 49
# Cursive Capitals *U* and *V*

**Lesson 49  Cursive Capitals** *U* **and** *V*

Reminders:
   Be sure the two slant lines of the letter *U* have the same slant.
   Be sure the double curve of the *V* is smooth and even.

The upland plover is a fairly large bird of the plains, with long legs, a long neck, a short bill, and a small head.
   Verdins are desert birds that can be seen around small desert bushes. They are smaller than sparrows, with a yellow head and a red patch on each wing.

*Copy the capital and small letter* 𝒰 *in the space following.*

𝒰 𝒰 𝒰 𝒰

𝓊

*Copy each word in the space following.*

𝒰pland                    𝒰nder

*Copy the capital and small letter* 𝒱 *in the space following.*

𝒱 𝒱 𝒱

𝓋

*Copy each word in the space following.*

𝒱erdin                    𝒱oices

| L.F. | 10 |
| Sl. | 10 |
| St. | 10 |
| Pr. | 10 |
| G.N. | 20 |
| L.S. | 10 |
| W.S. | 10 |
| Total |  |

*Copy the capital letters* 𝒰 *and* 𝒱 *three times each. Then write* 𝒰nto *and* 𝒱ery

103

## Aim of the Lesson

To teach the children the proper formation of the cursive capital letters *U* and *V*.

## Drill

Have the children practice the double curve in this drill session. It should be made smoothly and gracefully.

125

## Conducting the Class

1. Go over the explanation and demonstration for each of these letters. Show that the beginnings are similar but that the endings of these letters are different. The letter *U* ends more conventionally, with a slant-undercurve ending, but the letter *V* had a double-curve ending.

2. Have the children practice these letters on the blackboard or in the air prior to doing the lesson.

3. Go over "Reminders." Be sure the children understand the directions; then have them proceed with the lesson.

## Other Comments

1. The stroke combinations for the letters *U* and *V* are as follows:
   *𝒰*—loop, slant, undercurve, slant, undercurve
   *𝒱* —loop, slant, double curve

2. Be sure to call attention to the fact that the second part of the letter *U* does not rise as high as the first part.

3. Emphasize the points under "Reminders" as the children work the lesson.

## Practice Sentences

1. Upland plovers fly very stiffly.
2. Verdins' voices are high, thin whistles.
3. Verdins are in the bushtit family.

# Lesson 50
# Cursive Capitals *W* and *X*

**Lesson 50   Cursive Capitals *W* and *X***

Reminder:
  Remember to make the two parts of capital
*X* touch.

There are possibly more species of warblers
in North America than any other kind of bird.
But you probably will not see them as often as
some other kinds. These birds are shy and
most of them like to live deep in wooded areas.
  About the only bird whose name begins with
*x* is the xenops, a small bird of Central and
South America. Like the warbler, the xenops
lives deep in the forest.

*Copy the capital and small letter 𝒲 in the space following.*

*Copy each word in the space following.*

Warbler                    Wisdom

*Copy the capital and small letter 𝒳 in the space following.*

*Copy each word in the space following.*

Xenops                    Xerxes

L.F. 30
Sl. 10
Sz. 10
Pr. 10
G.N. 20
L.S. 10
W.S. 10
  Total

*Copy the letters 𝒲 and 𝒳 three times each. Then write the word Wonderful.*

105

## Aim of the Lesson

To teach the children how to make the cursive capital letters *W*
and *X* neatly and accurately.

## Drill

Have the children practice writing the word *Without* stroke by
stroke as you call each one out. The strokes are as follows: loop, under,
under, slant, over; under, slant, under, slant, under, slant, over, slant,

127

double, oval, under, slant, under, slant, under, slant, under, dot, cross, cross. Increase speed each time.

## Conducting the Class

1. Explain the formations of the letters *W* and *X* and demonstrate them on the blackboard as you explain. Both letters begin with a loop-undercurve combination. With the letter *X* the pencil is lifted between the first and second parts of the letter.

2. Have the children practice both of these letters in the air.

3. Go over "Reminder" and the directions with the children. Then have them proceed with the lesson.

## Other Comments

1. The stroke formations for the letters *W* and *X* are as follows:
    *W* —loop, undercurve, undercurve, slant, overcurve
    *X* —loop, undercurve, overcurve, undercurve

2. Be careful to ensure that the two parts of the letter *X* are touching.

3. Be sure the children understand the formation of the letter W and are able to make it properly without needing to look at a sample of the letter.

4. You may wish to mention that Xerxes (zûrk´ sez) was a Persian king. Many people think he is the same king as Ahasuerus of the Book of Esther.

# Lesson 51
# Cursive Capitals *Y* and *Z*

**Lesson 51  Cursive Capitals *Y* and *Z***

Reminder:
  Be sure the loops at the bottom of each letter are neither too wide nor too narrow.

The yellow-headed blackbird is about half black and half yellow. The head is a very bright yellow. It likes to live in marshy areas.
  The zone-tailed hawk has a wingspread of over one yard (over one meter). It eats small animals and other birds.

*Copy the capital and small letter Y in the space that follows them.*

*Copy each word in the space following.*
*Yellow-headed*                    *You*

*Copy the capital and small letter Z in the space that follows them.*

*Copy each word in the space following.*
*Zone-tailed*                    *Zoo*

Copy the letters *Y* and *Z* three times each. Then write *Yes* and *Zipper.*

107

## Aim of the Lesson

To teach the children to form the cursive capital letters *Y* and *Z* accurately and neatly.

## Drill

Have the children drill on the word *bright* stroke by stroke as you call the strokes out. The strokes are as follows: under, slant, under, retrace, under, under, slant, under, slant, double, oval, slant, double, slant, over, slant, under, slant, under, dot, cross.

129

## Conducting the Class

1. After drill, demonstrate the formations of both $Y$ and $Z$ while you explain the strokes. Both letters are full-height and also lower-loop letters. This makes them longer than most capital letters.

2. Following your demonstration, the children should practice both of these letters in the air.

3. Go over "Reminder" and the directions. Then have the children proceed with the lesson according to the directions.

## Other Comments

1. The stroke combinations for these letters are as follows:

   $\mathcal{Y}$ —loop, slant, undercurve, slant, overcurve

   $\mathcal{Z}$ —loop, undercurve, undercurve, overcurve

2. Be sure the children learn to make the long slant of the capital $Y$ straight from top to bottom. Call their specific attention to it.

3. The two sides of $Y$ should be consistently and accurately spaced.

4. Be sure the letter $Z$ maintains proper straightness. Although there are no slant lines in it, it should not look as though it were falling over either forward or backward. It should not look like this ( $\mathbf{\mathcal{Z}}$ ) or like this ( $\mathbf{\mathcal{Z}}$ ).

## Practice Sentences

1. Prairies are home to the yellow-headed blackbird.
2. Yellow-headed blackbirds like cattails.
3. Zone-tailed hawks live in northern Mexico.

# Lesson 52
# Alignment (Part 1)

**Lesson 52 Alignment** (Part 1)

Reminders:

Remember to make each letter as well as you can.

Take care that every letter sits exactly on the bottom line, not rising above or dropping below it.

*Alignment* means to make your letters straight—not straight up and down, but straight across. Your writing should look straight and even as it goes across the page.

One important part of alignment is to be sure each letter rests firmly on the bottom line. Even the letters that go below the line have a part that rests on the line.

Writing that goes above or below the bottom line looks sloppy. So let us be careful to always make each letter touch the bottom line at the place where it is supposed to.

*Copy this portion of Psalm 28:7 on the lines below.*

"The Lord is my strength and my shield; my heart trusted in him, and I am helped: therefore my heart greatly rejoiceth."

Write the words "With my song will I praise him" on the line below.

109

## Aim of the Lesson

To teach the children to keep their letters firmly attached to the base line in their writing.

## Drill

Have the children drill on the undercurve-slant combination, trying to ensure proper movement and smoothness on this critical and frequently used combination.

## Conducting the Class

1. Read over and discuss point by point the information at the top of the page. Keep chalk in hand to demonstrate each point.

2. Have the children practice writing the word *across* in the air, bringing every letter down to an imaginary base line.

3. After you go over "Reminders" and the directions, have the children proceed with the lesson. You should be careful not to let them deviate from the base line more than by the very smallest amount.

## Other Comments

1. Unless care is taken, some poor handwriting habits can be developed at this age. One  of these poor habits that often helps to cause illegibility several years later is not keeping one's writing firmly attached to the base line. Do not hesitate to curb this bad habit now.

2. **Al.** on the grading scale stands for *alignment*.

# Lesson 53
# Alignment (Part 2)

**Lesson 53  Alignment** (Part 2)

Reminder:
   Continue to watch the bottoms of your letters for alignment and also align the tops.

Another part of alignment is to make the parts of the letters that do not rest on the bottom line even. The tops of all the short letters should be even. The medium letters should be even. The tall letters should be even. And the bottoms of the lower-loop letters should be even.

One way you can tell if you have correct alignment in your writing is by drawing straight lines across the tops of your letters of each different height. If your lines have to curve to touch the tops of the letters, your alignment is not very good.

*This writing is not correctly aligned.*
Copy this sentence on the line below.
*This writing is properly aligned.*

Copy this sentence on the line below.
*Are you satisfied with your alignment?*

Copy each letter in the space following it.
*Y*                                                          *y*

L.F.   25
Sl.    10
Sz.    10
Pr.    10
G.N.   15
L.S.   10
W.S.   10
Al.    10
   Total

On the line below copy the sentence *"Oh, that men would praise the Lord!"*

111

## Aim of the Lesson

To teach the children to keep the tops and bottoms of their letters level and even.

## Drill

Have the children drill on the overcurve-slant combination. Emphasize a smooth execution of this stroke combination and proper arm movement.

## Conducting the Class

1. Go over the paragraphs at the top of the lesson page with the children. Demonstrate each point on the blackboard whenever possible. You should carefully explain just what letters and parts of letters should be even (see number 1 under "Other Comments").

2. Have the children practice writing the word *letter* in the air, making each letter meet imaginary alignment lines at the proper heights.

3. After going over "Reminder" and the directions, have the children proceed with the lesson.

## Other Comments

1. The letters and parts of letters that should be evenly aligned are as follows:

> first level: *a*, lower part of *b*, *c*, lower part of *d*, *e*, *g*, lower part of *h*, *i*, *j*, lower part of *k*, *m*, *n*, ovals of *p* and *q*, *u*, *v*, *w*, *x*, *y*, *z*
> first-plus level: (just above first level) *r*, *s*
> second level: *d*, *p*, *t*
> third level: *b*, *f*, *h*, *k*, *l* (plus all capital letters)
> 1½ level below: *f*, *g*, *j*, *q*, *y*, *z*

2. Alignment is closely related to proportion. Be sure the children's height proportion is correct. Especially be sure that *t*'s and *d*'s are not as tall as the upper-loop letters.

## Practice Sentences

1. "Verily God hath heard me." (Psalm 66:19)
2. "Our own God shall bless us." (Psalm 67:6)
3. "I will declare what he hath done for my soul." (Psalm 66:16)

# Lesson 54
# Cursive Capital *Q*

**Lesson 54  Cursive Capital** *Q*

Reminders:
    Remember to have your paper slanted properly and your fingers in a stretched-out position as you write.
    Be sure to make the final double curve of the letter *Q* very smooth and graceful.

Quails are heavy-set, chicken-shaped birds, but they are not nearly as large as chickens. They spend most of their time near the ground. Some of them have a long, curved feather on the top of their head. Quails include the familiar bobwhite whose clear call can often be heard early on a summer morning.

*Copy the loop-undercurve combination on the line below.*

*Copy the letter Q on these two lines.*

*Copy this sentence in the line below.*

*Quails often like to live in dry climates.*

*Copy the letter q to the end of this line.*

L F   25
SI    10
Se   10
Iv    10
G N  15
L N  10
W S  10
AI    10
    Total

*Copy the letter Q three times. Then write Quick, Question, and Quiet*

113

## Aim of the Lesson

To teach the children the proper formation of the cursive capital letter *Q*.

## Drill

Have the children drill on the double curve, learning to make it smoothly and gracefully. They can then put it to practice on the letter *Q*. As they make the double curve each time, say "curve, curve" to identify the two parts.

## Conducting the Class

1. Explain and demonstrate the formation of the letter *Q*. The children's first impression will be that it looks like the number *2*. There are similarities, but you should also point out the differences. The letter *Q* begins with a loop and ends with a double curve that goes below the line, but the number *2* does not.

2. After your careful explanation, the children should practice the letter *Q* in the air.

3. Go over "Reminders" and the directions; then have the children proceed with the lesson.

## Other Comments

1. The stroke formation of the letter *Q* is as follows:

$\mathcal{2}$—loop, undercurve, double curve

2. The letter *Q* can be very attractive if it is made fairly rapidly and with proper form. Encourage the children to make and join the strokes in the smoothest possible manner.

3. Continue to watch that the loops on the children's letters are correctly formed.

# Lesson 55
# Cursive Capital *D*

**Lesson 55  Cursive Capital** *D*

Reminders:
Remember to have your paper slanted properly.
Remember to make each letter rest firmly on
the bottom line.

Ducks are water birds that are often seen
swimming on ponds and quiet streams.
The mallard duck is one of the most common.
The male can easily be recognized by its bright-
green head and brown breast.
Some ducks dive deep under the water, looking
for food. You may think they will not come up
again, when suddenly you see them pop up three
yards away!

*Copy this double curve stroke combination to the end of the line.*

*Copy the letter* $D$ *on lines two and three.*

*Copy this sentence on the line below.*

Ducks do not all say "quack."

*Copy the letter* $d$ *in the space following.*

LF  25
Sl   10
Sz  10
Pr  10
G.N  15
L.S  10
W.S  10
Al   10
Total

*Copy the letter* $D$ *three times. Then write* Does, Dead, Did, *and* Dot.

115

## Aim of the Lesson

To teach the children to form the cursive capital letter *D* properly.

## Drill

Have the children drill on the word *Duck* after you have explained
the formation of the capital letter *D*. The strokes are as follows: double, double, under; under, slant, under, slant, double, over, under,
slant, over, under, slant, under.

137

## Conducting the Class

1. Explain and demonstrate the formation of the letter *D*. Be sure you are thorough and show just how each double curve and the under-curve are formed.
2. Have the children practice the letter *D* several times in the air.
3. Conduct "Drill" exercises (from above).
4. Go over "Reminders" and the directions, and have the children proceed with the lesson.

## Other Comments

1. The stroke formation of the letter *D* is as follows:
   *D*—double curve, double curve, undercurve
2. You will likely need to emphasize proper width with this letter. It is easy for the children to make the letter too squashed ( *D* ) or too wide ( *D* ).
3. The letter *D* needs to touch the bottom line twice. Do not allow the children to make letters like this ( *D* ).
4. The second double curve should not have sharp corners ( *D* ) but is to be as gently curved as possible ( *D* ).

## Practice Sentences

1. Ducks are smaller than swans and geese.
2. Down helps keep ducks warm and dry.
3. Ducks have webbed feet that make good paddles.

# Lesson 56
# Cursive Capital *E*

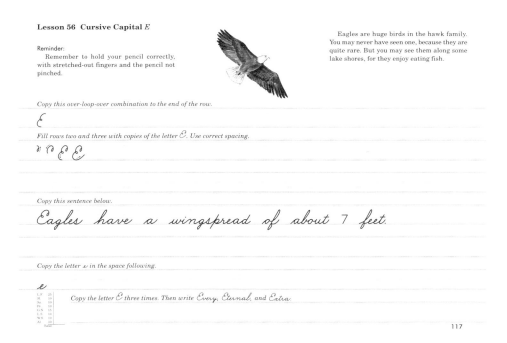

**Lesson 56  Cursive Capital** *E*

Reminder:
    Remember to hold your pencil correctly, with stretched-out fingers and the pencil not pinched.

Eagles are huge birds in the hawk family. You may never have seen one, because they are quite rare. But you may see them along some lake shores, for they enjoy eating fish.

*Copy this over-loop-over combination to the end of the row.*

*Fill rows two and three with copies of the letter* E. *Use correct spacing.*

*Copy this sentence below.*

Eagles have a wingspread of about 7 feet.

*Copy the letter* e *in the space following.*

*Copy the letter* E *three times. Then write* Every, Eternal, *and* Extra.

117

## Aim of the Lesson

To teach the children the proper formation of the cursive capital letter *E*.

## Drill

Following your explanation of the capital letter *E*, drill the children on the word *Eagle* as you call out the strokes. The strokes are as follows: loop, over, over, double, oval, slant, double, oval, slant, double, slant, under, (hook), slant, under.

139

## Conducting the Class

1. Explain and demonstrate the letter *E*. Every part of this letter is a curve. One needs to be extra careful to make every part correct when there are no slant lines to give the letter backbone.

2. Have the children practice the letter *E* in the air.

3. Conduct "Drill" (from above).

4. After explanation, practice, and drill, go over "Reminder" and the directions. Then have the children proceed with the lesson.

## Other Comments

1. The stroke formation of this letter is as follows:

*E* —loop, overcurve, overcurve, undercurve

2. Work on the backward loop, being sure the children give it the proper slant, length, and form.

3. The natural inclination is to give the capital letter *E* very little stroke form. It should look like this ( *E* ), not like this ( *E* ). Emphasize that there should be a noticeable corner between the loop and the first overcurve, and between the second overcurve and the undercurve.

4. Are you as a teacher making proper use of the grading chart? Do your students' grades make sense? If all are failing, or all getting very high marks, you are likely deducting too much or too little, unless you have an unusual class. Try to be as fair as possible in grading.

# Lesson 57
# Cursive Capitals *T* and *F*

**Lesson 57  Cursive Capitals *T* and *F***

Reminders:
  Remember, there is a difference between *T* and *F*. Never make one for the other or get them mixed up.
  Be sure to make the top part of these letters accurately.

Terns are shore birds that look something like gulls, but their bills are more pointed. They eat fish and insects, while gulls tend to eat dead things.
  Flycatchers include kingbirds, phoebes, and wood pewees. They live up to their name by catching flies and other insects. They catch them with a loud snap of the beak!

*Copy the letter T in rows one and two.*

*Copy each word in the space following.*

*Tern*                    *Tomorrow*

*Copy the letter F in rows four and five.*

*Copy each word in the space following.*

*Flycatcher*                    *Find*

L.F  25
Sl   10
St   10
Pr   10
O.N  15
L.S  10
W.S  10
Al   10
Total

119

## Aim of the Lesson

To teach the children the proper formation of the cursive capital letters *T* and *F*.

## Drill

The children should drill on the word *Faith* by strokes as you call them out. The strokes are as follows: loop, double; double, under, slant; over, oval, slant, under, slant, under, slant, under, slant, over, slant, under, dot, cross.

141

## Conducting the Class

1. Explain and demonstrate *carefully* the formation of the two letters *T* and *F.* Be sure to practice making them correctly ahead of time, as these letters are among the most commonly misformed of all letters. Explain the similarities and differences between the two letters.

2. Have the children practice both letters in the air.

3. Conduct "Drill" (from above).

4. Go over "Reminders" and the directions, and then have the children proceed with the lesson.

## Other Comments

1. The stroke combinations for these two letters are as follows:

    *T*—loop, double curve, double curve, undercurve

    *F*—loop, double curve, double curve, undercurve, slant

2. The top part of these letters should be made first. Some systems teach making the bottom part first, but we feel that it is simpler and more expedient to make the top of these letters first.

3. Work hard to achieve a consistent and neat formation of the upper part of these letters.

4. Be sure the children slant *T* and *F* properly. They are easily misslanted because of the predominance of double curves.

5. Be sure the loops of these letters stay high. It is easy to make them so low that they almost touch the bottom portion, but this makes the letter look awkward and it is not correct.

## Practice Sentences

1. Terns have forked tails.
2. The scissor-tailed flycatcher has a tail about 9 inches long.
3. Most flycatchers are olive or gray in color.

# Review of Form

**Lesson 58 Review of Form**

Reminder:
  Remember where to begin in making the various forms and letters. Do not start at the bottom of a form, for example, when you should start at the top.

*Copy each of these common stroke combinations in the space following at least three times.*

*Write each small and capital letter of the alphabet on the last four lines.*

Accuracy of Form  80
Quality        20
        Total

121

## Aim of the Lesson

To aid the children in reviewing basic stroke combinations and letter forms.

## Conducting the Class

1. Begin by discussing form—what it is and why it is important. We recognize most things because they have a particular shape. Look at the birds at the top of the page. You can recognize them by their

shapes. The blue jay has a crest, the swallow is thin with narrow wings and tail, and the duck has a wide, flat bill.

2. Letters have form like birds do. We recognize different letters by their proper form. If they are made improperly, we may not be able to recognize them. So we want to make them all properly.

3. Explain some of the errors in form that children often make. Letters like *a, d,* and *g* not being closed are errors in form. Demonstrate how they can be mistaken for other letters when not properly made (*a* for *u*, *d* for *il*, and g for *ij*). The letter *c* can be mistaken for *i* if it is not properly curved. The letters *t* and *l* can get mixed up if a loop is not made where it should be ( *low* ) or is made where it should not be ( *tow* ), especially if the letter *t* is not crossed. Demonstrate each of these. Have each child watch his own writing to prevent these errors from occurring.

4. The children should proceed with the lesson after you go over "Reminder" and the directions with them.

## Other Comments

1. Watch carefully and be sure the children correct any form errors that you see on their papers. Be sure they understand the proper method of writing the letter or letters that they made incorrectly, since improper methods will stick and become bad habits.

2. The end of the year is approaching. Evaluate your children's general progress in penmanship with a view to a final grade. Be sure to consider not only where they are, but how much they have improved since the beginning of the year.

# Lesson 59
# Review of Quality

**Lesson 59  Review of Quality**

Reminder:
  Do you remember the different kinds of quality
to look for and take care to make them a part of
your writing? They are slant, alignment, neatness,
size, proportion, letter spacing, word spacing, and,
this time, line quality.

*Copy this verse and sentence on the lines following, correcting each error as you write.*

*Be not wise in thine own eyes: fear the Lord, and depart from evil. Proverbs 3:7.*

*We need to realize that God knows much more than we do.*

123

## Aim of the Lesson

To review the nature of each area of quality; also, to teach how to recognize poor writing quality and correct it.

## Conducting the Class

1. Explain that the pictures at the top of the lesson are an illustration of quality in writing. As can be readily seen, the one bird is really healthy. It is fat and sleek, with its head held high. The other

145

bird is skinny, with coarse feathers and its head drooping down. The first bird is good quality. It has good form, size, and proportion. The second bird is poor quality in almost every way.

2. Like birds, there are healthy and unhealthy letters. Some are written neatly and carefully, with good slant, size, proportion, alignment, and so forth. These are healthy letters and they have good quality. Others are falling over, are too small, too big, too low, too high, or in some other way made improperly. These are "sick" letters, and they have poor quality like the unhealthy bird.

3. Would you enjoy birds if most of them were half-dead, could barely sing, could just totter around from place to place, would fall off limbs, and could hardly fly because they had so few feathers? Of course not! Neither should we enjoy making letters that are not beautiful and really healthy.

4. Go over the different areas of quality. Be sure the children understand just what is involved in each one. Draw attention to the "Reminder" section as you go over these areas of quality. Explain *line quality* (**L.Q.**) to the children, for example, writing too light or too heavy.

5. Explain the lesson directions. If you have time, it would be profitable to have the children draw short arrows pointing to each mistake in the original copy.

6. Have the children proceed with the lesson according to your instructions.

## Other Comments

1. Following is a list of mistakes in the original copy in the lesson:
   *Be*—*B* is too short
   Spacing is too wide between *Be* and *not.*
   *not*—*n* improperly slanted
         too much space between *o* and *t*
   *wise*—none
   *in*—too heavy
   *thine*—too small
   *own*—too big
   *eyes*—line quality too light, then too heavy
         extra marks on letter *y*
   *fear*—improper alignment

*the*—improper spacing

*Lord*—slant is too nearly vertical

Spacing is too close between *Lord* and *and.*

*and*—too much slant

Spacing between *and* and *depart* is too wide.

*depart*—extra marks on letter *a*

*from*—incorrect proportion

Word spacing is too close between *from* and *evil.*

*Proverbs 3:7*—none

*We*—*e* is too small

Word spacing is too wide between *we* and *need.*

Word spacing is too narrow between *need* and *to.*

*to*—too much slant

*realize*—improper alignment and proportion

*that*—inconsistent slant

*God*—none

*knows*—too small

*much*—too small

*more*—inconsistent letter spacing

*than*—line quality is too light

Word spacing is too close between last three words.

2.  Evaluate carefully the quality of the children's letters. Call each child's attention to any glaring errors in quality on his paper. Circle letters or words that need correction, and have the children write each correctly five times, as a means of test preparation.

3.  There will be no practice sentences in this lesson. The children should spend the time making corrections and preparing for the test.

# Lesson 60
# Final Test

**Lesson 60  Final Test**

1. Why must you be careful to write neatly?
_____

2. How should you hold your pencil when you are writing?
_____

3. How should you place your paper on your desk when you use slant print or write cursive?
_____
_____

4. How should you sit while you write?
_____

5. The basic strokes in cursive writing are named here. Make each one after its name.

   oval _____     slant _____     undercurve _____     overcurve _____     loop _____     double curve _____

6. Match each name with what it means.
   a. size            _____ how even a letter is across the top and the bottom
   b. alignment       _____ how nice your paper looks
   c. letter spacing  _____ the size of letters or letter parts compared to others
   d. word spacing    _____ the distance between letters in a word
   e. proportion      _____ the amount that letters lean
   f. neatness        _____ how big or small the letters are
   g. slant           _____ the distance between words

7. Write the following sentence in slant print and then in cursive:
   I will love Thee, O Lord, my strength.

## Conducting the Class

Be sure that the children understand the questions on the test; then have them proceed with it. Each child is to answer number 3 in a way that is right for *himself.*

## Answer Key

1. I must write neatly so that others can read what I have written. (other reasons possible)

2. Hold the pencil tightly enough to control it, but do not pinch it.
3. Slant the paper to the left (or to the right for left-handers).
4. Sit with your back straight. Lean forward only a little.
5. $O$ $/$ $\smile$ $\frown$ $\partial\sim$
6. b, f, e, c, g, a, d
7. Use the evaluation chart to score.

## Grading the Test

To properly grade the test, count numbers 1–6 as one-half of the test and number 7 as the other half. Each part of number 7 is one-fourth of the test. Deduct points for incorrect answers in numbers 1–6 and for poor form and quality in number 7.

This final grade should not count for the entire penmanship grade for the year. Average it in with other grades, but do it so that its value is several times greater than any other grade.

# Slant Print Stroke Formations

A B C D E F G H I

J K L M N O P Q R

S T U V W X Y Z

a b c d e

f g h i j k l m n o

p q r s t u v w x y z

1 2 3 4 5 6 7 8 9 0